ALSO BY PAULA DEEN

Paula Deen's My First Cookbook

Paula Deen's Kitchen Wisdom and Recipe Journal

Paula Deen: It Ain't All About the Cookin'

Christmas with Paula Deen

Paula Deen Celebrates!

The Lady & Sons Just Desserts

Paula Deen & Friends: Living It Up, Southern Style

The Lady & Sons, Too!: A Whole New Batch of Recipes from Savannah

The Lady & Sons Savannah Country Cookbook

PAULA DEEN'S

The Deen Family Cookbook

PAULA DEEN

with Melissa Clark

Photographs by Alan Richardson

SIMON & SCHUSTER

New York   London   Toronto   Sydney

SIMON & SCHUSTER
1230 Avenue of the Americas
New York, NY 10020

First Simon & Schuster hardcover edition April 2009

SIMON & SCHUSTER and colophon are registered trademarks
of Simon & Schuster, Inc.

For information about special discounts for bulk purchases,
please contact Simon & Schuster Special Sales at
1-866-506-1949 or business@simonandschuster.com.

The Simon & Schuster Speakers Bureau can bring authors
to your live event. For more information or to book an event
contact the Simon & Schuster Speakers Bureau at
866-248-3049 or visit our website at www.simonspeakers.com.

Designed by Dana Sloan

Photographer's Assistant: Roy Galaday
Food Stylist: Michael Pederson
Prop Stylist: Debrah E. Donahue

Manufactured in the United States of America

1   3   5   7   9   10   8   6   4   2

Library of Congress Cataloging-in-Publication Data

Deen, Paula H.
Paula Deen's: the Deen family cookbook / Paula Deen with Melissa Clark;
photographs by Alan Richardson.
p.   cm.
1. Cookery, American—Southern style.
I. Clark, Melissa. II. Title.
TX715.2.S68D493   2009
641.5975—dc22   2008049281
ISBN-13: 978-0-7432-7813-3
ISBN-10:   0-7432-7813-5

Frontispiece: (Back row) Anthony Groover, Jennifer Moesch, Bobby Deen, Aunt Peggy Ort, Jay Hiers; (middle row) Daniel Reed, Michael Groover, Paula Deen, Uncle Bubba Hiers; (bottom row) Michelle Reed, Corrie Hiers, Brooke Deen, Jamie Deen, Jack Deen.

This book is a celebration of family and is lovingly dedicated to my whole family, each and every member. I'm so grateful for your continued love and support; it's what makes everything possible and I love you all!

The same can be said for my extended family, meaning all the employees of our restaurants and company. Though we don't share the same blood, we do share the sweat (and sometimes tears) that goes into running our family business. Thank y'all for your loyalty and hard work!

And finally, I'd like to dedicate this book to all families across America. Whether related by blood or by love, you are truly the backbone of our great nation!

Acknowledgments

There are so many people to thank and acknowledge for this cookbook. And not just the people who actually worked on it, but the whole family of folks who help me run my business and enjoy my life, every single day.

My heartfelt thanks go out to my manager, Barry Weiner, who couldn't look out for me better if he was my own daddy. Thanks to my literary agent, Janis Donnaud, who has an eye for talent and a flair for matching up the very best people to do the very best work. Thanks to my fantastic editor, Sydny Miner, who is not only the sharpest knife in the drawer but has an absolutely inspiring amount of patience. And thanks to her crackerjack assistant, Michelle Rorke, and everybody at Simon & Schuster, especially publisher David Rosenthal. Thanks to art director Jackie Seow, photographer Alan Richardson, food stylist Michael Pederson, and prop stylist Deb Donahue, who have somehow made my simple home cooking look like regular works of art. Thanks to my collaborator, Melissa Clark, who coaxed these family recipes out of all of us Deens, Hiers, Groovers, and Orts when all the while she was cooking up an addition to her own family (congratulations on your sweet baby girl, Melissa!).

As always, I have to thank the brilliant Phyllis Hoffman and her hardworking staff who publish my beautiful magazine, *Cooking with Paula Deen*, and to all my friends at the Food Network, especially my pal Gordon Elliot. Thanks to my tireless personal assistants, Brandon Branch, Theresa Feuger, Hollis Johnson, and Sarah Meighen, who help make my busy schedule just as fun as can be. Thanks to my publicist, Nancy Assuncao.

And, of course, my gratitude goes out every day to my tried-and-true staff at The Lady & Sons, especially Dora Charles, Rance Jackson, Dustin Walls, and Scott Hopke. And thanks, also, to everyone at Uncle Bubba's Oyster House, especially Lisa Jackson.

And to all the rest of my darling family: my husband, Michael; my boys, Jamie and Bobby; my daughter-in-law, Brooke, and grandson, Jack; the Groover kids, Anthony and Michelle, and Michelle's husband, Daniel Reed; my baby brother, Bubba; my niece, Corrie, and my nephew, Jay; Michael's brothers, Father Hank and Nick; all the many dear cousins, aunts, and uncles; and to my beloved Aunt Peggy Ort. I hope you all know you mean the world to me.

And a special thank-you to all my fans—I love y'all and think of us as one great big, happy family.

Contents

Main Dishes 63

Breakfast and Brunch 163

Desserts and Sweets 195

Beverages **243**

PAULA DEEN'S

The Deen Family Cookbook

dried herb in place of one tablespoon of the fresh, as the dried herb has a more concentrated flavor. The same formula works in reverse. You can substitute one tablespoon of fresh chopped herbs for each teaspoon of dried.

Use peanut, vegetable, or soy oil for all the deep-frying recipes. Canola oil will not work as well for frying, but it does make an excellent salad oil. When a recipe calls for olive oil, I like to use extra-virgin olive oil, especially if it's for a dressing or other uncooked dish, though pure olive oil is just fine for sautéing.

Nibbles, Snacks, and Sandwiches

When my family comes over and I'm cooking, they always want something to snack on while they're waiting on me to finish up the meal. A good selection of nibbles keeps everyone from getting too hungry and it also prevents them from getting underfoot. Just set that plate of goodies wherever you want them and they're bound to follow it!

I have so much fun with making little snacks. For one thing, they free me up to be creative. I like to experiment a bit, and I figure when it comes to these kinds of things, you can put anything together. You know, when I prepare a meal, it's got to make sense to me. For example, I wouldn't serve spaghetti along with macaroni and cheese, and I always serve salad and Italian bread with my spaghetti. But with the hors d'oeuvres, you can go a little crazy. So if you feel like setting out a big old platter filled with mini quiches, fried pickled okra, and guacamole, I say go ahead—it's all good!

Serve a few of the simpler recipes when you've got folks over to watch the game, or make a bunch of the ritzier ones for a cocktail party. What they all have in common is loads of flavor in a small package—just the thing to get your taste

Opposite: Deep-Fried Pickled Okra with Creamy Chile Dip (page 16).

buds going. While I'm on the topic, have you ever wondered how to estimate just how many nibbles a person can put away? Well, if it's me and those little glazed wieners that Michael makes, you don't want to know! But seriously—most party planners say that before dinner you should serve around five bite-size nibbles per person; I find this holds true if you do plan on serving a meal. At a grazing type of party where the nibbles are the main event, figure ten to twelve bites per person per hour. Unless you've got a bunch of Deens coming over—in that case, double everything!

Twice-Baked Cheese Straws

One 4-ounce box cheese straws,
about 12 straws

¾ cup (3 ounces) grated Cheddar
cheese

Salt and pepper

Don't you just love cheese straws? I've made them myself, which is a heck of a lot of work, and you know what? The ones you can buy are just as delicious. But I hit on the perfect way to make them even better: more cheese, of course! I take store-bought cheese straws, melt cheese all over them, and serve them warm. You know they are goooood!

PAULA'S TIP: **Don't worry if you open up a box of straws and find they're broken. Just break all the straws into pieces before you put the cheese over them. Then go ahead and serve them in a bowl.**

MAKES ABOUT 12 STRAWS

1. Preheat the oven to 375°F. Line a baking sheet with greased waxed paper or a nonstick liner.

2. Arrange the straws on the baking sheet. Press the cheese onto the straws; sprinkle them with salt and pepper. Bake the straws for 10 minutes or until the cheese is golden and bubbling. Serve warm or at room temperature.

Tiny Sausage-Tomato Bites

1 pound bulk sausage (hot,
    sweet, or breakfast sausage),
    crumbled

3 cups baking mix, such as
    Bisquick

2 cups (½ pound) grated Cheddar
    cheese

24 cherry tomatoes, halved

Now these are cute and tiny, and they don't take much time to make, but that doesn't mean their flavor won't knock your socks off. The tomato in the center makes them prettier than the usual sausage ball.

MAKES 48 BITES

1. Preheat the oven to 375°F. In a medium bowl, combine the sausage, baking mix, and cheese. Mix very well with your hands or in a food processor, until the meat and cheese are evenly distributed (the mixture will seem dry). Roll and press the mixture into 1-inch balls.

2. Transfer the sausage balls to a baking sheet and flatten each one with the palm of your hand. Make a small indentation in each patty with your thumb and nestle a tomato half, cut side up, in the indentation.

3. Bake until the meat is cooked through, 15 to 25 minutes. Serve hot or warm.

Tiny Sausage-Tomato Bites (top) and Sweet
Surprise Cheddar-Olive Bites (bottom; page 14).

Sweet Surprise
Cheddar-Olive Bites

Baked Cheddar balls with an olive nestled inside have always been one of my favorite snacks. So my guests—while always delighted—are never surprised to see them show up at a party. This time, though, I thought I'd surprise them by stuffing those olives with a sweet bite of date. Salty, sweet, and crunchy, y'all, these are addictive!

PAULA'S TIP: **These are perfect for parties where you've got plenty else to worry about. The olives can be stuffed, wrapped, and refrigerated for up to one day prior to baking.**

MAKES 24 BITES

2 cups (½ pound) grated extra-sharp Cheddar cheese

4 tablespoons (½ stick) butter

1 cup all-purpose flour

¼ teaspoon cayenne pepper

24 pitted large green olives

6 pitted dried dates, quartered lengthwise

1. Preheat the oven to 400°F. Line two baking sheets with parchment paper.

2. In a food processor, combine the cheese, butter, flour, and cayenne; pulse until a smooth dough forms.

3. Fill each olive with a sliver of date. Mold 1 tablespoon of dough around each olive, covering it completely. Arrange the olives on the prepared baking sheets. Bake until golden, about 15 minutes. Serve warm.

Jamie's Jalapeño Bottle Caps with Blue Cheese Dip

DIP

½ cup sour cream

¼ cup mayonnaise

½ teaspoon salt

½ teaspoon pepper

½ cup (2 ounces) crumbled blue cheese

¼ cup finely chopped green onions (scallions), white and light green parts

BOTTLE CAPS

Peanut oil, for frying

½ cup Fry Mix (page 17)

6 tablespoons beer

3 jalapeño peppers (about 3½ ounces), trimmed and sliced crosswise ¼ inch thick, seeded if desired

Salt

Once you taste Jamie's blue cheese dip, you'll know he's consumed his fair share of buffalo wings. The cool, creamy dip is just right for putting out a fire in your mouth, and the fried peppers are just hot enough to keep you dipping!

PAULA'S TIP: **Buy fat jalapeños for this recipe so you get nice big slices to fry. If you can take the heat, leave in the seeds; otherwise, cut out those spicy little devils before you batter the peppers.**

MAKES ABOUT 24 PIECES

1. To make the dip, combine the sour cream, mayonnaise, salt, and pepper. Fold in the blue cheese and green onions. Cover and refrigerate until ready to use.

2. To make the bottle caps, heat the oil in a deep skillet to 375°F.

3. While the oil heats, combine the fry mix with the beer, stirring until smooth. Toss the jalapeño slices in the batter. Using a slotted wooden spoon or tongs, carefully lower the jalapeño slices into the oil. Fry, turning them often to brown evenly, for about 2 minutes. Drain on a paper towel–lined plate and season with salt. Serve immediately with the dip.

Deep-Fried Pickled Okra with Creamy Chile Dip

If you've had fried pickles, then you can guess how extra special this crispy fried pickled okra is, especially with a little of this rich, fiery dip. We always keep a jar of pickled okra in the pantry for snacking, so we can whip this up whenever the fried-food urge strikes, which is pretty much all the time at our place!

PAULA'S TIP: **Make up a batch of Fry Mix to have on hand so you can treat anyone who drops by to some down-home deep-fried nibbles. You can use it for almost anything fried, from green tomatoes to shrimp.**

MAKES ABOUT 24 PIECES

1. To make the dip, blend the cream cheese, mayonnaise, chipotles, lime juice, and salt in a food processor until smooth. Cover and refrigerate until needed.

2. To make the deep-fried okra, heat the oil to 375°F in a deep skillet. Combine the Fry Mix with the beer. Add the okra, coating it in the batter. Fry the okra about 4 pieces at a time, turning the pieces frequently, until golden brown, about 2 minutes. Transfer the okra to a paper towel–lined plate to drain. Serve immediately with the dip.

DIP

One 8-ounce package cream
    cheese, softened

2 tablespoons mayonnaise

1½ chipotles from a can of
    chipotles in adobo sauce

2 teaspoons freshly squeezed
    lime juice

¾ teaspoon salt

DEEP-FRIED OKRA

Peanut oil, for frying

1¼ cups Fry Mix (recipe follows)

1 cup beer

One 16-ounce jar pickled okra,
    drained

FRY MIX

MAKES 7 CUPS

6 cups self-rising flour (see Note)

1 cup self-rising white cornmeal (see Note)

1 teaspoon salt

1 teaspoon crushed black peppercorns

Whisk together the flour, cornmeal, salt, and pepper. Store in an airtight container in the pantry until needed.

NOTE: To substitute for 6 cups self-rising flour, use 6 cups all-purpose flour plus 3 tablespoons baking powder and 1½ teaspoons salt. To substitute for 1 cup self-rising cornmeal, use ¾ cup plus 3 tablespoons white cornmeal, 1 tablespoon baking powder, and ½ teaspoon salt.

PAULA'S TIP: **To deep-fry evenly, it's important to keep turning the food you're frying; otherwise, you won't get an even browning. They may not be traditional in the South, but wooden chopsticks work great for this.**

Bubba's Spicy Corn and Crab Puffs

A meal at Uncle Bubba's Oyster House is a close second to cracking crabs over at Bubba's house, but if you can't get to either place, you'll love my little brother's corny crab puffs. In fact, since the crabmeat is already out of the shell and you can just pop these in your mouth, I sometimes prefer them to a crab boil. There are times I'm just not in the mood to have to work at eating my dinner!

¾ cup buttermilk

2 eggs

One 8½-ounce box corn muffin
mix

1 pound lump or backfin
crabmeat, well drained and
picked clean of shells

1 cup frozen corn kernels,
thawed and drained

5 green onions (scallions),
white and light green parts,
trimmed and chopped

2½ teaspoons Paula Deen Hot
Sauce or other hot sauce,
plus more to taste

1 teaspoon salt, plus more to
taste

¼ teaspoon pepper, plus more to
taste

Peanut or vegetable oil, for frying

BUBBA SAYS: **Here in Savannah we've got crabs all in the creeks. I like to put out a crab trap and catch my own fresh blue crabs, then invite folks over on a Sunday afternoon. We have some cold beers and then figure out what we're going to do with all the crabs I caught. Well, this is one of the ways I like to eat them. Go ahead and try to eat just one; I swear you won't be able to stop.**

MAKES ABOUT 42 PUFFS

1. In a medium bowl, whisk together the buttermilk and eggs. Stir in the corn muffin mix. Fold in the crab, corn kernels, green onions, and hot sauce. Add the salt and pepper.

2. Heat the oil in a deep skillet to 330°F.

3. Using two spoons, carefully drop heaping tablespoons of the crab mixture into the oil and fry for 2 to 3 minutes, turning often for an even golden-brown color and crispness. Transfer to a paper towel–lined plate to drain. Season with additional hot sauce, salt, and pepper, if desired. Serve immediately.

Candied Bourbon-Bacon Bites

The name says it all, y'all. These things are so good, and so easy to make, they are about enough to get any party started.

MAKES ABOUT 36 BITES

¾ pound sliced bacon

2 tablespoons bourbon

½ cup packed light brown sugar

1. Preheat the oven to 350°F. Line a rimmed baking sheet with foil and place a wire rack on top.

2. Arrange the bacon strips close together in a single layer on the rack. Brush the strips generously with the bourbon. Sprinkle the brown sugar over the top.

3. Bake until crisp and dark golden brown, 20 to 25 minutes. Transfer the bacon strips to a wire rack set over a rimmed baking sheet or to a paper towel–lined plate to cool slightly. Break each strip into thirds and serve warm or at room temperature.

Aunt Trina's Shrimp Boulettes

1 pound large shrimp, peeled and deveined

1 large russet potato, peeled and very finely chopped

1 medium yellow onion, very finely chopped

4 green onions (scallions), white and light green parts, trimmed and chopped

3 tablespoons all-purpose flour

1 egg, lightly beaten

1 teaspoon salt, plus more to taste

½ teaspoon pepper

Peanut oil, for frying

My Aunt Trina is a wonderful cook, and now that she makes her home in Louisiana, she has gotten into all that fabulous Cajun and Creole cooking. This is a recipe that one of her neighbors shared with her.

AUNT TRINA SAYS: **We make these every year when shrimp season comes around. If they're shrimping, you've got to have your boulettes. Some folks make them and sell them on the street or at street fairs.**

MAKES ABOUT 36 BOULETTES

1. Grind the shrimp in a food processor to a coarse consistency. Add the potato and yellow onion and pulse just to combine. Transfer the mixture to a bowl.

2. Stir in the green onions. Fold in the flour and egg and add the salt and pepper.

3. Heat 2 inches of oil in a deep skillet over medium heat until the oil reaches 375°F on a deep-fat thermometer.

4. Working in batches, drop the shrimp mixture by the spoonful into the oil. Fry the boulettes until dark golden brown, about 5 minutes. Transfer to a paper towel–lined plate to drain. Season with salt and serve hot.

Mini Artichoke and Gruyère Quiches

These mini quiches are so sweet and dainty, you can stuff your face with them and still feel like a proper Southern lady.

MAKES 12 MINI QUICHES

1. Preheat the oven to 300°F. Grease a 12-cup mini-muffin tin with the softened butter.

2. In a small bowl, combine the cracker crumbs and melted butter, then divide the mixture evenly among the muffin cups, pressing the crumbs up the sides.

3. In a medium skillet over medium-high heat, brown the bacon for 5 minutes, turning once. Add the green onions and sauté for 3 minutes. Add the artichokes and cook for 2 minutes more. Crumble the bacon, allow the mixture to cool for 2 to 5 minutes, then divide it evenly over the cracker crumbs. Sprinkle the grated cheese over the artichoke mixture.

4. Beat together the milk, egg, salt, and pepper. Spoon the mixture into the muffin tin, filling the cups three-quarters full.

5. Bake the quiches until they are just set in the middle, 15 to 20 minutes, watching carefully so as not to overbake. Serve hot or warm.

NOTE: The quiches can be stored, covered, in the refrigerator for up to 3 days, or in the freezer for a month. Warm them in the oven before serving.

4 tablespoons (½ stick) butter, melted, plus 2 tablespoons (¼ stick) butter, softened

¾ cup crushed Ritz crackers (about 16 crackers)

4 slices bacon

1 tablespoon chopped green onions (scallions), white and light green parts

½ cup chopped marinated artichoke hearts

½ cup (2 ounces) grated Gruyère cheese

½ cup milk

1 egg

¼ teaspoon salt

⅛ teaspoon pepper

Ham and Chutney Biscuit Fingers

3 tablespoons minced mango chutney, like Major Grey's

3 tablespoons butter, softened, plus 3 tablespoons chilled butter

2 cups self-rising cake flour (see Note)

½ teaspoon baking powder

⅓ cup whole milk, plus more if needed

⅓ cup buttermilk

3 ounces thinly sliced ham

When you come to one of my family's parties and look for the finger food, this is what you're going to get! These biscuit fingers are always a hit.

MAKES 20 OPEN-FACED SANDWICHES

1. Preheat the oven to 400°F.

2. In a bowl, combine the chutney and softened butter until smooth. Set aside.

3. In a separate bowl, whisk together the flour and baking powder. Cut in the chilled butter until the mixture forms chickpea-size chunks. Stir in the milk and buttermilk. Drizzle in more milk, 1 tablespoon at a time, if needed to form a moist dough.

4. On a lightly floured surface, knead the dough just until it comes together. Pat it into an 8 by 5-inch rectangle, then cut that in half crosswise and cut each half lengthwise into fifths, making ten 2½ by ½-inch biscuit fingers.

5. Transfer the fingers to a baking sheet and bake for 10 to 15 minutes, until golden. Let cool for several minutes before slicing each in half crosswise, as you would a sandwich. Slather each half with chutney butter. Arrange, buttered side up, on a serving plate. Top with the ham slices and serve open faced.

NOTE: If you can't find self-rising cake flour, whisk together all-purpose flour, ½ teaspoon baking powder, and ¼ teaspoon salt for each cup you need.

Michael's Grilled Glazed Mini Dogs

I just love my own mini dogs, Otis and Sam, so much I could eat them up! Well, these here mini dogs are just as yummy! Seriously, everybody loves mini wieners—you just can't go wrong with them.

MAKES 30 TO 48 MINI WIENERS

2 tablespoons ketchup

2 tablespoons Dijon mustard

3 tablespoons apricot jam

½ teaspoon Paula Deen Hot Sauce or other hot sauce, or to taste

One 12- to 16-ounce package mini wieners (cocktail franks)

1. Light the grill or preheat the broiler to high. Whisk together the ketchup, mustard, jam, and hot sauce in a small bowl and set aside.

2. Arrange the mini wieners in a grill basket or on a baking sheet; brush them all over with glaze. Grill or broil the wieners for 2 minutes, then flip them and continue cooking for another 2 minutes, watching carefully to see that they don't burn. Brush with more glaze and serve.

Corrie's Sausage, Herb, and Cream Cheese Crescent Rolls

4 ounces cream cheese (half of an 8-ounce package), softened

2 teaspoons chopped fresh sage

½ pound bulk breakfast sausage, crumbled

¼ teaspoon Paula Deen Hot Sauce or other hot sauce

One 8-ounce tube refrigerated crescent rolls

We just love to dress up crescent roll dough in our family. Bubba's kids, Corrie and Jay, are particular fans. It's so satisfying to have something warm and fresh coming out of the oven, especially when it takes no effort. Corrie's rolls have been the subject of more than a few family spats—we tend to feel that one batch is never quite enough, so these days, she always doubles it to keep the peace.

CORRIE SAYS: **These are great to eat when they're hot, but they're just as good after they've cooled down. What I really like to do is make them if I have to get up early to go to see a game or something. Last year I made them when we all went to see the St. Patrick's Day parade. We ate them for breakfast, and took them along to snack on for lunch.**

MAKES 8 ROLLS

1. In a small bowl, stir together the cream cheese and sage until well mixed. In a skillet over medium-high heat, brown the sausage until cooked through, 5 to 7 minutes, breaking it up with a fork as you go; stir in the hot sauce. Let cool.

2. Preheat the oven to 375°F. Remove the crescent roll dough from the tube and open the dough triangles so they lie flat. Spread the cream cheese over each one. Top each triangle with an even layer of sausage. Roll the dough into a crescent according to the package directions and transfer to a baking sheet. Bake until golden, about 15 minutes. Serve warm or at room temperature.

Paula's Perfect Pickled Shrimp and Eggs

Oh, I just love these. In the South, you'll see these big ol' beautiful jars of pickled eggs at the curb store (some folks call them convenience stores) and there is just nothing better. They'll sell you an egg in a piece of waxed paper and you eat it right then and there. And since Michael got me into eating pickled shrimp, one day I just combined the two.

PAULA'S TIP: **I love to pick up beautiful antique jars at yard sales to show off my pickled eggs.**

SERVES 12

2 cups apple cider vinegar

1½ cups white vinegar

1 small yellow onion, sliced

1 tablespoon mustard seeds

1 tablespoon sugar

1 teaspoon Paula Deen Hot Sauce
   or other hot sauce

1 teaspoon salt

2 bay leaves

½ pound large shrimp, peeled
   and deveined

12 hard-boiled eggs, peeled

1. In a saucepan, combine the vinegars, onion, mustard seeds, sugar, hot sauce, salt, and bay leaves. Bring to a boil, then reduce the heat and let simmer for 5 minutes. Add the shrimp and cook until just opaque, about 2 minutes.

2. Place the eggs in a large, very clean jar (or use two jars) and pour in the hot liquid and shrimp. Seal the jar(s) and refrigerate for at least 24 hours, or longer if you like more pickle to your egg.

Elegant Stuffed Eggs with Smoked Salmon

12 eggs

¼ cup sour cream

2 tablespoons mayonnaise

2 tablespoons chopped fresh chives, plus extra for garnish

1½ teaspoons prepared horseradish

1 teaspoon apple cider vinegar

½ teaspoon pepper

6 ounces smoked salmon, cut into ¼-inch strips

These are just some good deviled eggs all dressed up for a party with a topping of smoked salmon. If you think no one can resist regular deviled eggs, just wait until you put a platter of these babies out for the taking. You'd better have backup because, I promise, they go fast.

MAKES 24 PIECES

1. Place the eggs in a medium pot and cover with cold water. Bring to a boil over high heat. Immediately remove the pot from the heat, cover it, and let stand for 10 minutes. Uncover the pot and let the eggs cool in the water.

2. Peel the eggs and cut them in half lengthwise. Pop out the yolks into a bowl. Arrange the whites on a platter. Mash the yolks well with a fork or press them through a sieve. Combine the yolks with the sour cream, mayonnaise, chives, horseradish, vinegar, and pepper. Spoon or pipe the filling into the eggs.

3. Roll each strip of salmon into a tight coil. Arrange these salmon rosettes on top of the yolks. Sprinkle with chives and serve.

Bobby's Hot Tomato, Jack, and Crab Dip

Bobby makes crab dip like nobody's business. The cheesy, creamy, spicy, salty smoothness hits your mouth all at the same time, and it's chock-full of fresh crabmeat. I could not improve upon his recipe if I tried!

SERVES ABOUT 8

One 8-ounce package cream
  cheese, softened

1 cup (4 ounces) grated pepper
  Jack cheese

½ cup mayonnaise

2 tablespoons freshly squeezed
  lime juice

1 teaspoon Paula Deen Hot Sauce
  or other hot sauce

1 pound lump crabmeat, well
  drained and picked clean of
  shells

1 cup seeded, diced tomatoes
  (2 medium tomatoes)

¼ cup chopped green onions
  (scallions), white and light
  green parts

¼ cup chopped fresh basil

2 cloves garlic, finely chopped

¼ teaspoon salt

½ teaspoon crushed black
  peppercorns

2 avocados

Crackers or crusty bread, for
  serving

Uncle Bobby and Jack.

1. Preheat the oven to 350°F. In a large bowl, mix together the cream cheese, pepper Jack, mayonnaise, lime juice, and hot sauce until smooth. Fold in the crabmeat, tomatoes, green onions, basil, garlic, salt, and pepper.

2. Smooth the mixture into a 1-quart baking dish. Bake until golden and bubbly, about 30 minutes.

3. Split, pit, peel, and dice the avocados and sprinkle them over the crab dip after it has cooled slightly. Serve warm with crackers or crusty bread.

Jodi's Cream Cheese and Shrimp Dip

My sister-in-law Jodi Groover (Michael's younger brother Nick's wife) is a great addition to our family, and so is her dip! If you've never had shrimp dip, you are in for one big treat. You can serve this as a spread with toast or crackers, or throw in a little more sour cream for something chip-ready and divine.

JODI SAYS: **This may not look like many ingredients, but mix it all up and let it sit in the fridge for 8 hours and it tastes like you spent all that time working on it.**

MAKES ABOUT 2 CUPS DIP

Mix the shrimp, cream cheese, green onions, sour cream, mustard, and hot sauce well. Cover and refrigerate for at least 8 hours before serving.

14 ounces peeled and deveined cooked shrimp, finely chopped

One 3-ounce package cream cheese, softened

¼ cup finely chopped green onions (scallions), white and light green parts

2 teaspoons sour cream

2 teaspoons Dijon mustard

½ teaspoon Paula Deen Hot Sauce or other hot sauce

Crackers, crusty bread, or raw vegetables, for serving

George IV's Favorite Guacamole

George Ort is my Aunt Peggy's oldest. He was always smart growing up, and because I was five years older, I thought he was quite a little know-it-all. I remember once when I was sixteen and didn't know squat except how to dress for a date and do my cheer, we had a little incident in the car.

You see, I had this old convertible. It was my first car that my daddy had given me, and for some reason I had George, his brother, Paul, and my brother in the car with me and I wasn't happy about it. Well, when little George in his smart way said, "I could drive this car better than you," I turned around and said, "You think so, you little smart aleck?" Then I pulled over and said, "Okay, drive it, big boy."

Oh, my God! He got behind that wheel and he was all over the road and up on the curb and I remember just dying laughing. Back then things were so innocent, you know—you would never do that today. But that was the beauty of the small town. I just laughed and laughed and I said, "Obviously you can't drive as good as I can." I remember the two younger boys just screaming! They just knew we would be killed. I was full of devilment back then. So I got back behind the wheel and I never did tell none of the adults what I had done.

Well, now George is a successful executive and his wife, Kelley, is one of those perfect mothers and wives. I've never seen her without makeup, and I've never seen her without the perfect meal on the table. She's just one of those girls that you aspire to be like, and she's a fabulous cook. And now, it turns out, so are her teenage sons, George IV and T.J. Don't you just love it when good things run in the family?

5 ripe avocados, pitted and peeled

1 large tomato, chopped

1 small yellow onion, finely chopped

½ cup chopped cilantro

Finely grated zest of 1 lime

3 tablespoons freshly squeezed lime juice

2 cloves garlic, finely chopped

1 jalapeño pepper, seeded and finely chopped (about 2½ teaspoons)

1 teaspoon salt, plus more to taste

Tortilla chips, for dipping, or lettuce, for salad

KELLEY SAYS: **George IV perfected this recipe after watching a friend demonstrate how easy it is to make this super-fresh dip. He went on to win the "guacamole throw-down" contest at a recent Super Bowl party.**

MAKES 1 QUART GUACAMOLE

Mash the avocados in a large bowl. Stir in the tomato, onion, cilantro, lime zest and juice, garlic, jalapeño, and salt. Cover tightly and refrigerate for 1 hour to bring out the flavor. Serve with tortilla chips or on top of lettuce as a salad.

Michelle's Corny Pimiento Cheese Sandwiches

Pimiento cheese is a staple of the South and everyone loves it in sandwiches, spread on crackers, or set out as a dip. It's hard to improve on the basic recipe, but our beautiful daughter Michelle managed to do so by stirring in some sweet corn for flavor and texture. You'll love it.

4 ounces cream cheese (half of an 8-ounce package)

2 cups (8 ounces) grated Cheddar cheese

½ cup mayonnaise

½ cup chopped pimientos, drained

1 teaspoon chopped yellow onion

1 small clove garlic, chopped

¼ teaspoon Dijon mustard

¼ teaspoon salt, plus more to taste

Pepper

½ cup frozen corn kernels, thawed and drained

8 to 12 slices white bread, for serving

(Clockwise) Anthony Groover; his girlfriend, Jennifer Moesch; Michelle Reed.

MICHELLE SAYS: **As a kid I swear we used to eat sticks of cream cheese like they were Snickers bars; that's probably why these sandwiches are one of my favorites. Everybody likes them, kids and adults. I tend to make them for parties like wedding or baby showers, when I know my friends will bring their kids.**

MAKES 4 TO 6 SANDWICHES

1. In a food processor, pulse the cream cheese until smooth. Add the Cheddar cheese, mayonnaise, pimientos, onion, garlic, mustard, salt, and pepper to taste, and pulse until just combined.

2. Scrape the cheese mixture into a bowl and fold in the corn kernels. Spread between slices of white bread to make sandwiches. Cut into halves or quarters and serve.

Appetizers, Soups, and Salads

I don't know about you, but when I go out to eat I form my opinion of the place by the very first bite they set down in front of me. If it's as simple as bread and butter, that's fine, but if that bread is disappointing, I figure there's a good chance the meal will be, too. But if that restaurant has done its best with the bread basket and served up a tasty green salad or lovely bowl of soup, I take it as a great sign that all the details of the rest of the meal will be looked after, too.

I believe it's just as important to set the stage when you're cooking at home, so I love to put together a crisp salad or a satisfying soup whenever I have the chance, even for a weekday supper. I always relish a good rice salad that you can make in advance, and Michael and I love to make slow cooker soups because they are just so hearty and convenient. Then there are those meals that call for something a little extra deluxe—that's when I break out my recipe for Beefy French Onion Soup (page 54) or Michael's Buttery Crab Potpies (page 58). And there are plenty of times when I like to make a soup or salad so hearty that I can serve it all by itself for a light lunch.

Your first course doesn't have to be a big production, just a little something delicious that makes you hungry for more, because at my house, there's *always* more!

Caesar Salad with Parmesan Crisps

A lot of people say they don't like anchovies, but I adore them. They give my Caesar dressing the right salty taste without being too fishy. And y'all know me, I just have to liven up my dressing with a few dashes of hot sauce, too. Along with the Parmesan crisps, which are basically just crunchy fried cheese, this winds up being one very exciting salad.

SERVES 6

1. To make the crisps, sprinkle the cheese by the tablespoon into a nonstick skillet over medium heat. Cook until lacy, and slightly set, about 1 minute. Flip the cheese and cook until crisp, about 2 minutes more. Transfer to a wire rack to cool.

2. To make the dressing, combine the olive oil, anchovies (if using), lemon juice, garlic, hot sauce, mustard, Worcestershire sauce, salt, and pepper to taste in a blender or food processor. Blend until smooth.

3. To assemble the salad, place the lettuce, eggs, and tomatoes in a large bowl and crumble in the Parmesan crisps. Pour enough dressing on the salad to coat well, toss, and serve.

CRISPS

¾ cup (3 ounces) grated
   Parmesan cheese

DRESSING

½ cup extra-virgin olive oil

4 anchovy fillets, rinsed and
   patted dry (optional)

2 tablespoons freshly squeezed
   lemon juice

2 cloves garlic

3 dashes of Paula Deen Hot Sauce
   or other hot sauce, or to taste

1 teaspoon Dijon mustard

½ teaspoon Worcestershire sauce

¾ teaspoon salt

Pepper

SALAD

2 hearts of romaine lettuce,
   chopped

3 hard-boiled eggs, peeled and
   quartered

1 cup cherry tomatoes, halved

Beet, Goat Cheese, and Arugula Salad with Pecans

1 pound beets, trimmed and scrubbed

3 bunches (12 ounces) arugula, rinsed and dried, thick stems cut off

⅓ cup chopped toasted pecans

3 tablespoons extra-virgin olive oil

1 tablespoon freshly squeezed lemon juice

Salt and pepper

¾ cup (3 ounces) soft goat cheese, crumbled

I love good beets, even straight out of the can. That sweet, earthy taste is exactly right matched up with smooth, tangy goat cheese and some gutsy salad greens like arugula. You can enjoy this salad anytime, it's so simple, but it's also elegant enough to serve as a first course for a special dinner.

SERVES 4 TO 6

1. Preheat the oven to 400°F. Wrap the beets tightly in a large sheet of foil and place on a rimmed baking sheet. Bake for 45 minutes to 1 hour, until the beets are tender when pierced with the tip of a knife.

2. Once the beets are cool enough to handle, peel, dice, and transfer them to a large bowl. Add the arugula and pecans; toss to combine.

3. In a small bowl, whisk together the oil, lemon juice, and salt and pepper to taste. Pour the dressing on the salad and toss well. Sprinkle the goat cheese on top and serve.

Paula's Italian Pasta Salad

I like my pasta salad a little on the sweeter side and loaded with everything I can get my hands on. In fact, this salad is a perfect way to clean out your refrigerator—just throw in whatever cheese and veggies you have. With the bow-tie pasta, I think it looks awfully pretty in a nice big salad bowl.

SERVES 6 TO 8

1. In a large pot of boiling salted water, cook the pasta according to the package directions.

2. While the pasta is cooking, in a small bowl, whisk together the balsamic vinaigrette, mayonnaise, and sugar.

3. Drain the pasta well, transfer to a large bowl, and allow to cool. Add the tomatoes, mushrooms, olives, green pepper, onion, and basil. Pour the dressing over the salad and toss to combine. Sprinkle in the cheese, toss lightly, and serve.

1 pound bow-tie pasta

1 cup store-bought balsamic vinaigrette dressing

¼ cup mayonnaise

1 tablespoon sugar

2 cups cherry tomatoes, halved

One 4-ounce can sliced mushrooms, drained

²/₃ cup pitted kalamata olives

¹/₃ cup diced green bell pepper

¹/₃ cup finely chopped red onion (1 small)

2 tablespoons chopped fresh basil

2 cups (8 ounces) crumbled feta cheese

Warm Bacon Vinaigrette over Greens

¼ pound (6 slices) bacon

1 tablespoon minced red onion

½ cup white wine vinegar

1 tablespoon Dijon mustard

Salt and pepper

Mixed greens, for serving

This dressing is out of this world. You toss it over greens when it's warm just to soften them a bit, without fully cooking them. And it's got enough bacon in the dressing to seduce any salad haters you may know—they won't be able to resist that smell of frying pork.

MAKES ⅓ CUP VINAIGRETTE, TO SERVE 4 TO 6

1. In a large skillet over medium heat, brown the bacon for 5 to 7 minutes, until crisp. Transfer the bacon to a paper towel–lined plate to drain, then crumble.

2. Add the onion to the skillet with the bacon grease and cook, stirring, over medium heat for about 1 minute, until softened.

3. In a small bowl, whisk together the vinegar and mustard. Add the mixture to the skillet and cook, stirring, for 1 minute. Stir in the bacon and season with salt and pepper to taste. Pour over the greens and serve.

Orange, Strawberry, and Date Salad with Buttermilk Dressing

DRESSING

6 tablespoons buttermilk

1 tablespoon freshly squeezed lemon juice

2 teaspoons finely chopped shallot

½ teaspoon chopped fresh tarragon

¼ cup vegetable oil

Salt and pepper

SALAD

1 head Boston lettuce, rinsed, dried, and torn into pieces

2 medium navel oranges

1 pint strawberries, hulled and quartered

½ cup pitted dates, thinly sliced crosswise

W hip up a bowl of this light and refreshing beauty anytime you want to make salad a little more special than just plain greens. It's just so perfect for brunch on a hot summer day, it'll perk you right up!

SERVES 4

1. To make the dressing, whisk together the buttermilk, lemon juice, shallot, and tarragon. Slowly whisk in the oil. Season to taste with salt and pepper.

2. In a bowl, coat the greens with all but ¼ cup of the dressing. Arrange the greens on individual serving plates.

3. Cut off the top and bottom of each orange, just exposing the flesh. With a sharp knife, follow the curve of the fruit to cut away the peel, completely removing the white pith. Slice out each segment of fruit, cutting in along the membrane. Divide the oranges, strawberries, and dates among the greens. Drizzle each serving with the remaining dressing.

Picnic-Perfect Ham and Rice Salad with Toasted Almonds

This is the prettiest picnic salad, with ham, peppers, olives and basil for color, and almonds for crunch. Better yet, the taste of it just gets more delicious as it sits, so bring it along for the ride, and by the time you reach your picnic spot, you're in for such a treat!

SERVES 8 TO 10

1. In a medium pot, combine the rice with 3 cups water and ½ teaspoon of the salt. Bring to a boil, then reduce to low heat, cover, and simmer for 20 minutes. Remove the pot from the heat and let stand, still covered, for 10 minutes. Fluff the rice with a fork, then let it cool, uncovered.

2. In a medium skillet over medium heat, toast the almonds until golden, tossing occasionally, 3 to 4 minutes.

3. In a small bowl, whisk together the lemon juice, mustard, the remaining ½ teaspoon salt, and the pepper. Whisk in the oil gradually, tablespoon by tablespoon.

4. In a large bowl, toss the rice with the dressing, almonds, ham, red pepper, olives, basil, and onion. Taste and adjust the seasonings. Serve warm or at room temperature.

2 cups long-grain white rice

1 teaspoon salt, plus more to taste

½ cup slivered almonds

1 tablespoon freshly squeezed lemon juice

2½ teaspoons Dijon mustard

½ teaspoon pepper, plus more to taste

6 tablespoons extra-virgin olive oil

½ pound thick-cut cooked ham, diced

¾ cup diced red bell pepper

½ cup pitted kalamata olives, thinly sliced

⅓ cup chopped fresh basil

¼ cup finely chopped red onion (½ small)

Jamie's Southwestern Avocado and Black Bean Salad

½ cup chopped cilantro

¼ cup extra-virgin olive oil

2 tablespoons freshly squeezed
  lime juice

2 or 3 dashes of Paula Deen Hot
  Sauce or other hot sauce

4 cups chopped romaine lettuce

2 avocados, pitted, peeled, and
  diced

2 cups fresh or frozen corn
  kernels, thawed (if frozen)
  and drained

Two 15-ounce cans black beans,
  rinsed and drained

1 cup chopped cherry tomatoes

About ¾ cup (3 ounces) grated
  pepper Jack cheese

Salt and pepper

Chock-full of beans, avocado, corn, and cheese, you can really sink your teeth into this salad. Whenever Jamie says he'll fix a salad, I know I'd better save up an appetite, because that boy means business.

SERVES 4

1. In a small bowl, whisk together the cilantro, oil, lime juice, and hot sauce.

2. In a large bowl, combine the lettuce, avocados, corn, beans, tomatoes, and cheese. Add the dressing and toss well. Season with salt and pepper and serve.

Hoppin' John Salad

Traditionally served on New Year's Day in the South, Hoppin' John is a big ol' mess of rice and black-eyed peas. Well, I think that winning combination is just too delicious to break out only once a year, so I started making it as a salad for our family picnics in the summertime. It's always popular, and makes a great dish for vegetarians.

PAULA'S TIP: **The rice will need more seasoning the more it sits, so be sure to taste and sprinkle in some salt and pepper right before you serve it.**

SERVES 4 TO 6

1. In a small bowl, whisk together the garlic, oil, and lemon juice.

2. In a large bowl, combine the rice, peas, green pepper, green onions, and parsley. Add the dressing and toss well. Season with the Tabasco, salt, and pepper to taste, toss again, and serve.

1 clove garlic, minced

3 tablespoons extra-virgin olive oil

2 teaspoons freshly squeezed lemon juice

2½ cups cooked long-grain white rice, cooled

One 15-ounce can black-eyed peas, rinsed and drained

1 small green bell pepper, seeded and diced

3 green onions (scallions), white and light green parts, trimmed and finely chopped

¼ cup chopped fresh parsley

1½ teaspoons Tabasco or other hot sauce

1 teaspoon salt

Pepper

Corrie's Creamy Corn and Shrimp Chowder

6 ears corn, kernels cut off the cobs, cobs reserved

2 tablespoons (¼ stick) butter

1 medium yellow onion, chopped

2 cups chicken broth

½ cup heavy cream

Salt and pepper

1 pound large shrimp, peeled, deveined, and cut into 1-inch pieces

3 green onions (scallions), white and light green parts, trimmed and chopped

Corrie is so special to me, and it just warms my heart to see her getting busy in the kitchen. She makes her chowder on the lighter side, filled with shrimp and corn, but not too thick—just like I like it.

CORRIE SAYS: **I always think of this as a fall dish, when the corn is at its peak, and, of course, our local shrimp are just the best. My mother used to serve this to me and my brother, Jay, in sourdough bread bowls, which we loved.**

SERVES 6 TO 8

1. Put the corn cobs into a large pot with just enough water to cover (break the cobs in half if they don't fit). Boil gently for 20 minutes. Discard the cobs and reserve the corn-infused water.

2. In a medium saucepan, melt the butter over medium heat. Add the onion and cook, stirring occasionally, until softened, 3 to 5 minutes. Add the corn kernels, chicken broth, cream, and 3 cups of the corn water. Season with salt and pepper to taste and bring to a boil. Lower the heat and let simmer for about 10 minutes. Add the shrimp and simmer until just opaque, 2 to 3 minutes.

3. Ladle the chowder into soup bowls and garnish with the green onions. Serve hot.

Tomato-Basil Soup with Blue Cheese Toasts

I decided to gussy up the old tomato soup and grilled cheese combo, and I think I hit on a winner. I make this for lunch on rainy days, and I swear the sun starts shining before we're done.

SERVES 4 TO 6

1. To make the soup, melt the butter in a large pot over medium heat. Add the onion and a pinch of salt. Cover and cook over low heat until very soft, about 15 minutes. Add the tomatoes and 4 cups water and increase the heat to medium-high. Simmer, uncovered, for about 30 minutes.

2. Puree the soup in batches in a food processor or blender, and return the mixture to the pot. Add the cream, season with salt and pepper, and stir in the chopped basil.

3. To make the toast, preheat the broiler with the rack 6 inches from the heat source. Place the bread slices on a baking sheet. In a small bowl, mash the cheese and butter together to make a paste. Broil the bread until golden, about 1 minute. Remove the bread from the oven, flip it, and spread the cheese mixture on top. Broil until the spread has melted and the edges of the toast are golden, 30 seconds to 1 minute. Reheat the soup if necessary and serve with the toast.

SOUP

3 tablespoons butter

1 medium Vidalia onion, very thinly sliced

Salt

One 28-ounce can diced tomatoes, undrained

¾ cup heavy cream or whole milk

Pepper

¼ cup finely chopped fresh basil

TOAST

6 slices white bread, cut in half diagonally

½ cup (2 ounces) crumbled blue cheese

1 tablespoon butter, softened

Kelley's Green Chile Taco Soup

3 tablespoons vegetable oil

1 pound ground beef

1 cup chopped yellow onion (1 large)

One 28-ounce can diced tomatoes, undrained

One 14-ounce can corn kernels, undrained

One 14-ounce can black beans, undrained

2 cups beef broth

One 4-ounce can chopped green chiles, undrained

1 teaspoon ground cumin

½ bunch cilantro leaves (about ¾ cup)

¼ cup sliced green onions (scallions), white and light green parts

½ teaspoon salt, or to taste

½ teaspoon pepper, or to taste

Grated Cheddar or Monterey Jack, for serving

George IV's Favorite Guacamole (page 34), for serving

Tortilla chips, for serving

Sour cream, for serving

This is a great meal that Kelley and George and the kids can all agree upon. There's so much in it, there's something for everybody.

KELLEY SAYS: **This recipe appeals to young and old alike and can easily be made for large crowds. You can adjust the spiciness by using either mild or hot chiles or by adding chili powder if you like it hot. We especially like this hearty soup on cold winter evenings after skiing and snowboarding. It is great served with tortilla chips and George IV's Favorite Guacamole (page 34).**

SERVES 6

1. Heat the oil in a skillet over medium-high heat. Brown the beef and onion, 7 to 10 minutes. Using a slotted spoon, transfer to a paper towel–lined plate to drain.

2. Scrape the beef mixture into a large pot over medium heat and add the tomatoes, corn, beans, broth, chiles, and cumin. Simmer for 15 minutes or until heated through. Turn off the heat and stir in the cilantro and green onions. Let stand for 10 minutes. Season with the salt and pepper. Reheat slightly and serve topped with cheese, guacamole, tortilla chips, and sour cream.

Beefy French Onion Soup

This is French comfort food in a bowl, all covered with cheese. The first time I had it, I knew I was going to have to try making it myself, because this is a soup I want to eat a lot more often than I find myself at a French restaurant. I add cubed beef, which makes it even heartier, and suitable for a main course if you serve it with French bread and a big salad. And, of course, when they're in season, I use big, sweet Vidalia onions; they give the broth the richest, most delicious flavor.

SERVES 4 TO 6

4 large Vidalia onions (about 2½ pounds), thinly sliced

4 tablespoons (½ stick) butter, melted

2 teaspoons sugar

2 tablespoons olive oil

¾ pound beef stew meat, cut into ½-inch cubes

¼ cup dry sherry

4 cups beef broth

2 teaspoons Worcestershire sauce

1 teaspoon salt

½ teaspoon dried thyme

1 bay leaf

Pepper

2 cups (8 ounces) grated Gruyère cheese

1. In a slow cooker, toss the onions with the butter and sugar. Cook, covered, on high, until the edges begin to brown, about 90 minutes.

2. In a large skillet over medium-high heat, warm the oil until shimmering, about 1 minute. Add the beef and brown, stirring occasionally, 5 to 7 minutes. Transfer the beef to the slow cooker. Add the sherry to the skillet and scrape up the browned bits. Add the pan juices to the slow cooker along with the broth, Worcestershire sauce, salt, thyme, bay leaf, and pepper to taste. Simmer, covered, for 2½ hours on high or 7 hours on low.

3. Uncover and simmer for 1 hour more, until thick. Remove the bay leaf.

4. When ready to serve, turn on the broiler. Ladle the soup into flameproof bowls and divide the cheese over the tops. Place the bowls on a baking sheet and broil until the cheese is melted and bubbling, about 3 minutes. Serve hot.

Michael's Navy Bean and Ham Hock Soup

1 pound dried navy beans, soaked overnight or by quick-soak method (see Note)

6 cups vegetable or chicken broth

1 or 2 smoked ham hocks

1 large yellow onion, finely diced (about 1 cup)

2 large carrots, finely diced (about ½ cup)

2 stalks celery, finely diced (about ½ cup)

2 cloves garlic, finely chopped

1¼ teaspoons salt

1 teaspoon pepper

¾ teaspoon Worcestershire sauce

½ teaspoon Paula Deen Hot Sauce or other hot sauce

The minute I learned that Michael's kids grew up loving his ham hocks and beans, I just insisted he make them for me, and I'm glad I did. He learned the recipe from a tugboat captain from North Carolina, and it's a keeper.

SERVES 4

1. Combine all the ingredients in a slow cooker. Cook, covered, until the beans are tender, about 4 hours on high or 8 hours on low. Uncover and cook for 1 hour more, until thickened.

2. Transfer the ham hock to a cutting board. Remove all the meat and fat from the bone; chop the meat into pieces and return it to the slow cooker. Serve hot.

NOTE: To use the quick-soak method, pick through the beans, discarding small stones or other foreign material. Put in a large pot (the beans will expand to two or three times their size). Add 8 cups water, bring to a boil, and boil hard for 3 minutes. Remove from the heat and let stand, covered, for 1 hour. When you can crush a bean between your fingers, they are ready.

Michael's Buttery Crab Potpies

Could I be any luckier than to have found me a man who makes crab potpies that just melt your heart, they're so delicious? This looks like some pretty fancy cooking, but it couldn't be easier to put together.

SERVES 4

8 tablespoons (1 stick) butter

1 small yellow onion, chopped

2 tablespoons all-purpose flour

1½ cups milk

¼ cup clam juice

¼ cup medium-dry sherry

½ pound crabmeat, well drained and picked clean of shells

Two 4-ounce cans sliced mushrooms, drained

1 cup frozen peas

2 sheets frozen puff pastry, thawed

1 egg, beaten with 1 teaspoon water

1. In a medium pot over medium heat, melt the butter. Add the onion and cook, stirring occasionally, until softened, 3 to 5 minutes. Sprinkle in the flour and cook, stirring constantly, for 1 minute. Add the milk, clam juice, and sherry. Bring to a boil and cook, stirring, until thickened, about 2 minutes. Add the crabmeat, mushrooms, and peas; remove from the heat and transfer to the refrigerator to cool.

2. Meanwhile, unfold the pastry sheets on a lightly floured surface. Place four ovenproof bowls or large ramekins rim down on the pastry and cut out four circles a bit larger than the bowls (you might need to roll the pastry out a bit to accommodate all the bowls). Preheat the oven to 350°F with a rack in the middle position.

3. When the crab filling has cooled, divide it among the four bowls. Brush the rims of the bowls with the egg mixture, lay a pastry circle over each, and seal the edges. Cut steam vents in the pastry and brush with the egg mixture. Place the bowls on a baking sheet and bake on the middle rack until the pastry is puffed and golden, 20 to 25 minutes. Serve hot.

Spicy Salmon and Corn Cakes with Mango Tartar Sauce

TARTAR SAUCE

1 cup peeled, diced mango
  (1 large)

½ cup mayonnaise

2 tablespoons capers, drained
  and chopped

Pinch of salt

Pepper

SALMON CAKES

One 14.75-ounce can boneless
  pink salmon, drained

1 cup panko (see Note), or dry
  bread crumbs

2 eggs, lightly beaten

3 tablespoons chopped fresh
  parsley

2 tablespoons chopped red onion

½ teaspoon cayenne pepper, or
  to taste

¼ teaspoon salt

Pepper

⅓ cup cornmeal

Vegetable oil, for frying

Michael and me in the outdoor kitchen.

These crispy salmon cakes are so full of flavor they make your mouth water for more, which is exactly what I'm looking for in an appetizer.

MAKES TWELVE 2-INCH CAKES AND 1½ CUPS SAUCE

1. To make the tartar sauce, whisk together the mango, mayonnaise, capers, and salt in a medium bowl. Add pepper to taste. Cover and refrigerate until ready to use.

2. To make the salmon cakes, put the salmon in a medium bowl and break it up with a fork. Add the panko, eggs, parsley, onion, cayenne, salt, and pepper to taste, and mix well. Form the mixture into 12 cakes and coat them with the cornmeal.

3. Heat ¼ inch of oil in a large skillet over medium-high heat. Carefully place the cakes in the oil 5 or 6 at a time, and cook until golden brown, 3 to 4 minutes per side. Transfer to a paper towel–lined plate to drain. Serve immediately with the tartar sauce.

NOTE: Panko is a Japanese style of bread crumbs and has a lighter, fluffier texture than the more familiar type. You can find it in large supermarkets.

Main Dishes

As much as I love snacks, appetizers, salad, and dessert (and y'all know how much I love dessert), when it comes to a meal, nothing beats the main event. It's the main course that everyone will remember, whether it's as simple as Michael's Slow Cooker Chicken 'n' Dumplings (page 74) for a casual Sunday supper, or maybe something fancier for a dinner party such as my Pan-Fried Pork Chops with Blackberries (page 88).

But just because it takes center stage doesn't mean you have to slave right up until serving time to put your main course on the table. Plenty of nights, I just like to keep it simple with my darling niece Corrie's Lemony, Buttery Baked Fish (page 65). And y'all know, I never miss an opportunity to throw everything in the slow cooker and let that machine do my cooking for me. My beef stew, full of mushrooms and beer (page 87), and Stewed Garlicky Sausage and Peppers (page 97) are so stuffed with flavor they taste like you spent all day, when really the slow cooker did. You may as well give yourself time to get cleaned up and put your feet up before sitting down to enjoy your meal!

Of course, when we're really celebrating, we do like to serve one of our extra special dishes, like my Corn Bread–Stuffed Crown Roast of Pork (page 91). But you can still give yourself a break by doing everything you can ahead of time, then just popping it into the oven before your guests arrive. And, you know,

Opposite: Shrimp Scampi with Artichokes and Basil (page 67).

if you set out a nice salad with your meat, and a store-bought dessert, no one would ever dare complain. Honey, being invited to someone's house for dinner is such a privilege that nobody cares if you snuck out and bought a nice pie at your favorite bakery.

You know what my favorite part of doing a nice dinner is? The leftovers! If my boys don't eat everything in sight or make off with whatever they couldn't finish, you'll find me making leftover sandwiches for lunch the next day. And don't tell, but some nights I like to sneak down for a midnight snack, and you know nothing makes me happier than finding some cold chicken in the fridge.

Kelley's Easy Grilled Shrimp

2 cloves garlic, minced

¾ teaspoon paprika

½ teaspoon cayenne pepper

½ teaspoon Old Bay seasoning

2 tablespoons olive oil, plus
    more for brushing the grill

2 pounds large or jumbo shrimp,
    peeled and deveined

1 teaspoon salt

Juice of 1 lemon

Lemon wedges, for serving

On nights when most moms are reaching for a box of macaroni and cheese, my cousin Kelley fixes her family a beautiful platter of shrimp in no time. That woman is an inspiration to me!

KELLEY SAYS: **We love to have friends over for casual outdoor dinners in the summer. To make entertaining a breeze, each summer we choose two or three easy menus and then repeat them with different groups of friends. This recipe has become an all-time favorite because it requires so little prep time and cooks so quickly once our guests arrive, not to mention how much everyone enjoys it! We just add a salad and some bread for a great meal.**

SERVES 4

1. Combine the garlic, paprika, cayenne, Old Bay, and the 2 tablespoons oil. Pour the mixture over the shrimp and marinate in a covered bowl or resealable plastic bag in the refrigerator for 30 minutes.

2. Lightly oil the grill grate and preheat the grill, or turn the broiler to high. Toss the shrimp with the salt and lemon juice; marinate for an additional 5 minutes. Grill or broil the shrimp for 2 to 3 minutes per side, until they are pink with some charring around the edges. Serve hot with lemon wedges.

Southern-Style Fish Boil

½ pound (2 sticks) butter

4 teaspoons Old Bay seasoning

¼ cup chopped fresh parsley

¼ cup salt

2 cloves garlic, finely chopped

1 pound small red potatoes, scrubbed

4 medium yellow onions, peeled, trimmed, and quartered through the root end

2 pounds white lake fish such as perch, cut into 1½-inch pieces

4 ears corn, husked and cut into thirds

A big ol' Low-Country boil might be stuffed full of sausage and seafood, but I recently learned how to make a meal that's just as delicious with little more than some nice fresh fish and corn: a Wisconsin fish boil. The first time I had this dish, I was visiting in Dorr County, Wisconsin, the heart of fish boil country. The lake fish there, served up with potatoes and corn, is so fresh and tasty that all it needed was plenty of melted butter and salt for seasoning. Let me tell you, I couldn't stop eating it! We love this style of cooking for family get-togethers out by the creek at Bubba's house. Everything goes in the same pot, and then we dump it out on a platter and everyone has at it.

PAULA'S TIP: **It's not called a boil for nothing. Make sure the water stays at a true boil while everything's cooking.**

SERVES 6

1. Melt the butter in a small saucepan over medium heat. Stir in the Old Bay and parsley. Set aside and reheat just before serving.

2. In a large pot, bring 1 gallon water to a boil with the salt and garlic. Add the potatoes; cook until almost tender, about 15 minutes. Add the onions; boil for 5 minutes. Add the fish; boil for 3 minutes. Add the corn; boil for 5 minutes more.

3. Using a slotted spoon or a long-handled strainer, transfer all the ingredients to a platter. Serve with the seasoned butter on the side for drizzling.

Bubba's bringing dinner home!

Michael's Deluxe Twice-Baked Potatoes with Shrimp

I tell you, some nights when we sit down to dinner, I just know Michael and I are a match made in heaven. Have you ever seen a potato stuffed with more delicious things than this?

SERVES 4

1. Preheat the oven to 450°F. Rub the potatoes with vegetable oil and place them on a baking sheet. Bake the potatoes until tender, about 1 hour.

2. While the potatoes are baking, cook the bacon in a skillet over medium-high heat for about 7 minutes, until crisp. Transfer the slices to a paper towel–lined plate to drain, then crumble them. Pour off all but 3 tablespoons of bacon grease from the skillet.

3. Cut the shrimp into thirds. Reheat the grease over medium-high heat. Add the shrimp, Cajun seasoning, and a pinch of salt; cook until the shrimp are opaque, stirring constantly, 2 to 3 minutes.

4. When the potatoes are done, let them cool slightly (leave the oven on). Slice off the top third of each potato and carefully scoop out the flesh into a bowl (scoop out the potato from the top third, too—you'll add that to the bowl— then discard the skin), leaving a ¼-inch border of potato inside the skin. Mash the potato flesh with 1 teaspoon salt, the green onions, butter, sour cream, mayonnaise, and pepper. Stuff the potato skins with the filling, mounding any extra on

Four 6- to 8-ounce russet potatoes, scrubbed and pricked all over with a fork

Vegetable oil, to coat potatoes

4 slices bacon

½ pound large shrimp, peeled and deveined, tails removed

1½ teaspoons Cajun seasoning

Salt

⅓ cup thinly sliced green onions (scallions), white and light green parts; chop the dark green parts for garnish

4 tablespoons (½ stick) butter, softened

¼ cup sour cream

3 tablespoons mayonnaise

¾ teaspoon pepper

top. Divide the shrimp on top of the potatoes and cover with the crumbled bacon.

5. Return the potatoes to the oven on the baking sheet and bake them until heated through, 5 to 10 minutes. Sprinkle with the reserved chopped green onions and serve.

Michael's Slow Cooker Chicken 'n' Dumplings

I had my recipe for chicken 'n' dumplings, and nobody ever complained, but when Michael moved in, well, you know, he had me beat. It's only fair that I share his recipe with y'all.

MICHAEL SAYS: **Believe it or not, I actually make a better chicken and dumplings than Paula, but I don't make it so much anymore. I'm scared to bring it out because she's just a little bit touchy when you can cook better than her.**

SERVES 4

One 3½-pound chicken, cut into 8 pieces

4 sprigs fresh parsley

4 stalks celery with leaves, chopped

2 carrots, peeled and chopped

1 medium yellow onion, cut into chunks

3 teaspoons salt

¼ teaspoon pepper

2 bay leaves

1½ cups plus 3 tablespoons all-purpose flour

2 teaspoons baking powder

½ cup milk

2 tablespoons vegetable shortening, melted

1 teaspoon chopped fresh parsley

3 tablespoons butter, softened

1. Put the chicken in a 3- to 5-quart slow cooker. Add water to cover, about 3 cups. Add the parsley sprigs, celery, carrots, onion, 2½ teaspoons of the salt, the pepper, and bay leaves. Cook for 3 hours on high or for 7 hours on low, until the meat falls from the bone.

2. In a bowl, combine the 1½ cups flour, the baking powder, and the remaining ½ teaspoon salt. In a separate bowl, combine the milk and shortening; stir the liquid into the dry ingredients. Fold in the chopped parsley. Drop the dumplings by tablespoons into the chicken broth. Cover the slow cooker and simmer on low for 40 to 45 minutes, until tender and cooked through.

3. Using a slotted spoon, transfer the dumplings to a bowl; transfer the chicken to another bowl. Once it's cool enough to handle, separate the chicken meat from the skin and bones

and discard the skin and bones. Strain the broth into a medium saucepan and discard the vegetables.

4. Mix the butter and the 3 tablespoons flour to form a paste. Bring the broth to a simmer over medium heat. Whisk in the paste and let simmer until thick, 2 to 3 minutes. Add the chicken to the sauce; then spoon the mixture over the dumplings to serve.

Corrie's Thai-Style Chicken and Veggies

We love Thai food in our house, and Corrie does such a scrumptious sauce for her chicken that I told her we had to write down the recipe and pass it along.

CORRIE SAYS: **This is a dish that really fills you up. I just love cooking with Asian spices, and I love the combination of sweet and spicy!**

SERVES 4

3 tablespoons olive oil

1 medium yellow onion, chopped

1½ pounds boneless, skinless chicken breasts, cut crosswise into strips

Salt and pepper

2 cups chicken broth

1 cup unsweetened coconut milk (*not* cream of coconut)

1 cup broccoli florets

8 ears canned baby corn, cut crosswise in half

½ cup drained canned sliced bamboo shoots

1 tablespoon sweet chili sauce

1 tablespoon Asian fish sauce (see Note)

Juice of ½ lime

1 tablespoon cornstarch

Cooked rice, for serving

1. In a medium saucepan, warm the olive oil over medium heat. Add the onion and cook, stirring occasionally, until softened, 3 to 5 minutes. Add the chicken, season with salt and pepper, and cook until just done, 5 to 7 minutes. Remove the chicken and reserve.

2. In the same pan, combine the broth, coconut milk, broccoli, baby corn, bamboo shoots, chili sauce, fish sauce, and lime juice. Boil gently until the broccoli is just tender, 3 to 4 minutes.

3. Meanwhile, in a small cup, combine the cornstarch with 1 tablespoon water and stir until smooth. Add the cornstarch to the pan and let boil, stirring, until slightly thickened, about 1 minute. Add the chicken and simmer until heated through. Serve with rice.

NOTE: Asian fish sauce is an aromatic and intensely flavored condiment generally made from fermented anchovies, salt, and water. Because of its strong taste, it should be used in moderation to give a subtle kick to Asian-inspired dishes. It is available in the international section of large supermarkets and on the Internet.

Bobby's Baked Chicken with Dijon and Lime

There's nothing that makes me feel better than sitting down to a dinner that one of my boys has cooked. Bobby does me proud with his healthy weeknight suppers—he's always got a flavorful twist on your basic chicken recipe to keep things interesting. I just loved this combination of mustard and lime the first time he made it, so he wrote down the recipe for me.

PAULA'S TIP: **If you just love lime, sprinkle a little more fresh lime zest on top of the chicken as a garnish just before serving.**

SERVES 4

One 3½-pound chicken, cut into 8 pieces

3 tablespoons Dijon mustard

1 tablespoon mayonnaise

1 clove garlic, minced

Finely grated zest and juice of 1 lime

¾ teaspoon pepper

Salt

Chopped fresh parsley, for garnish

1. Preheat the oven to 400°F. Rinse the chicken and pat dry; place in a large bowl. In a small bowl, whisk together the mustard, mayonnaise, garlic, lime zest and juice, and pepper. Season the chicken generously with salt. Pour the mustard-mayonnaise mixture over the chicken, tossing well to coat.

2. In a large baking pan, arrange the chicken to fit in a single layer. Bake until it is cooked through; breasts will take about 30 minutes, and legs will need 5 to 10 minutes more. Serve the chicken with the pan juices drizzled over the top and garnished with chopped parsley.

Country-Fried Chicken Livers with Chipotle Cream Gravy

CHICKEN LIVERS

½ cup all-purpose flour

1 tablespoon salt, plus more to taste

1 tablespoon paprika

½ teaspoon cayenne pepper

Pepper

2 pounds chicken livers

6 tablespoons vegetable oil, for frying

GRAVY

3 tablespoons all-purpose flour

2 cups hot whole milk

1 teaspoon salt, plus more to taste

¾ teaspoon Tabasco chipotle pepper sauce

½ teaspoon pepper, or to taste

Oh, I do love livers and gizzards; I just fry them right up! When you cook as much chicken as I do, you need yourself a good recipe for the rest of the bird. And honestly, y'all, anything would taste good smothered in this delicious gravy.

SERVES 4

1. To prepare the chicken livers, combine the flour, salt, paprika, cayenne, and pepper to taste in a medium bowl. Dredge the chicken livers in the flour mixture, tapping off the excess. Season with more salt and pepper, if desired.

2. Heat the oil in a large skillet over high heat. Fry the chicken livers, turning them once, until golden on both sides and still slightly pinkish inside, 1 to 2 minutes per side. Transfer the chicken livers to a paper towel–lined plate to drain.

3. To make the gravy, pour off all but about ¼ cup of the oil from the skillet. Return the skillet to medium-high heat. Add the flour and stir until browned, about 1 minute. Slowly whisk in the milk and cook, stirring constantly, until thick and bubbly, 2 to 3 minutes; stir in the salt, Tabasco, and pepper. Taste and adjust the seasoning if necessary. Spoon the gravy over the chicken livers and serve immediately.

Aunt Peggy's Old-Fashioned Meat Loaf

My Aunt Peggy came up with this meat loaf recipe for me back when I was making meat loaf sandwiches for The Bag Lady; it was always popular, and I never did improve on it.

AUNT PEGGY SAYS: **I put tomato paste and green pepper in this recipe because I just like to see a little color when I cut open my meat loaf.**

SERVES 4 TO 6

1 pound ground beef

One 6-ounce can tomato paste

½ cup chopped Vidalia onion

½ cup chopped green bell pepper

½ cup quick-cooking oats

1 egg, lightly beaten

1 teaspoon salt

¼ teaspoon pepper

⅓ cup ketchup

2 tablespoons packed light brown sugar

1 tablespoon Dijon mustard

1. Preheat the oven to 375°F. In a large bowl, combine the ground beef, tomato paste, onion, green pepper, oats, egg, salt, and pepper. Shape the mixture into a loaf and place it in a 9 by 5-inch loaf pan.

2. In a small bowl, whisk together the ketchup, brown sugar, and mustard. Slather the glaze on top of the meat loaf and bake for 1 hour or until the meat loaf is firm and cooked all the way through. Serve hot.

Michael's Company's Coming Grilled Steak and Veggie Supper

1½ tablespoons soy sauce

1 tablespoon Dijon mustard

2 cloves garlic, minced

1½ teaspoons dried oregano

1 teaspoon The Lady & Sons House Seasoning (page 66)

¾ cup vegetable oil

2 pounds flank steak

2 medium zucchini, cut into 1½-inch chunks

1 large red bell pepper, seeded and cut into 1½-inch chunks

1 large Vidalia onion, cut into 1½-inch chunks

Michael is most comfortable cooking outside, so we built him an outdoor kitchen in our backyard. He made this for company a couple of times, and I've been trying to figure out how to get him to make it just for me ever since.

SERVES 4 TO 6

1. In a large bowl, whisk together the soy sauce, mustard, garlic, oregano, and House Seasoning. Slowly whisk in the vegetable oil until fully incorporated. Transfer one third of the marinade to a separate bowl.

2. Add the steak to the remaining marinade. Cover and let sit for at least 1 hour and as long as overnight, refrigerated.

3. Thread the vegetables on metal or bamboo skewers (if you are using bamboo skewers, soak them in water for 30 minutes prior to use).

4. Light the grill or preheat the broiler. Grill or broil the steak, turning once, for 4 to 5 minutes per side for medium rare. Transfer the steak to a serving platter to rest.

5. Meanwhile, brush the vegetables with the reserved marinade and grill or broil them, turning once, for 10 minutes or until tender. Slice the steak and serve with the vegetable skewers.

Tybee Grilled Rib Eye with Fried Oysters

Tybee is our beach here on the Atlantic Ocean, and it is so quaint. All the locals march to the beat of their own drummer, so you know I feel right at home there. Well, I got this recipe from a wonderful restaurant on Tybee Island called The Sundae Café, and it is so yummy. If you want to go all out, serve it along with Southern Buttermilk Biscuit and Blue Cheese Bread Pudding (page 135).

SERVES 4

HOLLANDAISE SAUCE

4 egg yolks

½ cup heavy cream

4 tablespoons (½ stick) butter, cut into pieces

Juice of 1 lemon

Pinch of salt

Pinch of sugar

2 tablespoons white vinegar

¼ pound tasso ham, andouille sausage, or Spanish chorizo, diced

OYSTERS

¾ cup buttermilk

16 shucked oysters, drained and patted dry

¾ cup all-purpose flour

Pinch of paprika

Pinch of salt

Pinch of pepper

Vegetable oil, for frying

Four 14-ounce bone-in rib-eye steaks

Salt and pepper

1. To prepare the hollandaise sauce, in the top of a double boiler over barely simmering water, combine the egg yolks, cream, butter, lemon juice, salt, and sugar. When the butter has melted, whisk the mixture until thick, 3 to 5 minutes. Remove it from the heat and stir in the vinegar and ham.

2. To prepare the oysters, in a medium bowl, pour the buttermilk over the oysters. In a shallow bowl, combine the flour with the paprika, salt, and pepper. In a heavy pot, heat 3 inches of vegetable oil to 375°F. Lift the oysters out of the buttermilk, letting any excess drip off, and dredge them in the seasoned flour. Fry them in batches, turning them often, until golden, about 1 minute. Transfer to a paper towel–lined plate to drain.

3. Meanwhile, prepare the grill. Season the steaks with salt and pepper and grill them over hot coals for 5 minutes per side, until the outside has a nice char and the inside is rare to medium rare. Let the steaks rest for 5 minutes. Top each steak with 4 oysters and a big dollop of hollandaise.

Michael's Coffee-Braised Short Ribs

This easy slow cooker recipe is so luscious you wouldn't think it had such humble roots, but the inspiration comes from red eye gravy, that cowboy special where you fry up a steak, then throw a cup of old coffee in the skillet to make a deep, dark, flavorful sauce. And I just love short ribs: They don't cost much, and if you give them the time to cook, they turn out so tender and juicy you'll think someone just served you a filet mignon. We like to make this for a family dinner when the weather is a little nippy out. I send my boys home with the leftovers, and they swear they taste even better the next day.

3 pounds short ribs

Salt and pepper

2 tablespoons olive oil

1 cup dry white wine

1 cup strong brewed coffee

1 large yellow onion, chopped

3 cloves garlic, chopped

2 teaspoons hot or mild chili powder

1 teaspoon dried oregano

PAULA'S TIP: **If the sauce is too thin for your taste, strain the ribs out and simmer the sauce in a large saucepan until thick, then spoon it over the ribs and serve.**

SERVES 4 TO 6

1. Season the short ribs with salt and pepper. Warm the oil in a large skillet over high heat; brown the ribs, turning them once, until golden, about 8 minutes. Transfer the ribs to a paper towel–lined plate. Pour the wine and coffee into the skillet; cook over high heat, scraping up the brown bits, for 2 to 3 minutes, until the sauce is reduced by one fourth.

2. Place the ribs, onion, garlic, 2 teaspoons salt, the chili powder, and oregano in a slow cooker. Pour the wine-coffee sauce over the mixture. Cook, covered, for 3½ hours on high. Uncover and cook until the ribs are falling apart, 45 minutes more.

Stick-to-Your-Ribs Beef, Onion, and Mushroom Stew

3 pounds beef stew meat, cut into 1½-inch cubes

6 tablespoons (¾ stick) butter

3 tablespoons all-purpose flour

1 teaspoon salt

¾ teaspoon pepper

10 ounces mushrooms, quartered

2 large Spanish onions, halved and thinly sliced

One 12-ounce bottle dark beer

3 cloves garlic, minced

2 tablespoons packed light brown sugar

2 tablespoons Dijon mustard

1 tablespoon freshly squeezed lemon juice

3 sprigs fresh thyme

2 bay leaves

2 whole cloves

I made a lot of beef stew when the boys were growing up, and the recipe just settled into this one. Occasionally I'll use lamb to mix things up, and you could throw in some carrots if you like, but the heart of this recipe is the beer and mushrooms. It's a nice hearty meal in a bowl, perfect for a chilly night at home.

SERVES 6

1. In a large skillet, working in batches if necessary, brown the beef with 2 tablespoons of the butter over high heat, 5 to 7 minutes. Transfer the beef to a slow cooker and toss it with the flour, salt, and pepper.

2. Melt another 2 tablespoons of butter in the skillet and cook the mushrooms, turning them once, 1 to 2 minutes per side. Transfer the mushrooms to the slow cooker and toss them with the beef.

3. Melt the remaining 2 tablespoons of butter in the skillet and cook the onions for about 3 minutes, until softened. Transfer the onions to the beef mixture. Pour the beer into the skillet and simmer, scraping up the brown bits from the bottom of the pan. Pour the beer over the beef mixture and stir in the garlic, brown sugar, mustard, lemon juice, thyme, bay leaves, and cloves.

4. Cook for 8 hours on low. Remove the bay leaves and serve hot.

Pan-Fried Pork Chops with Blackberries

This is a beautiful summer supper that's fancy enough for company but simple enough for rushed weeknights. Whenever I eat blackberries I'm reminded of the days when me and Bubba were around the house all summer as children, just helping out some and getting into trouble more. We loved to go pick blackberries down the road, but you had to keep an eye out—if you even thought you saw a snake in those brambles, you grabbed your berry pail and hightailed it home.

Keep your sides simple; I love smashed boiled new potatoes and steamed green beans.

SERVES 4

Eight 6-ounce, ¾-inch-thick bone-in pork chops

The Lady & Sons House Seasoning (page 66), or salt and pepper

4 tablespoons (½ stick) butter

¼ cup canola oil

½ cup dry white wine

2 cups blackberries

1 tablespoon honey

1 tablespoon fresh thyme leaves

Lemon wedges, for serving

1. Sprinkle the chops with a generous amount of seasoning. Heat a large skillet over high heat. Add the butter and oil and swirl until the butter is melted. Sear the chops, in two batches if necessary, until golden, about 2 minutes per side. Transfer the chops to a paper towel–lined plate.

2. Remove the skillet from the heat, add the wine, and return it to the heat. Simmer, scraping up the brown bits, until the wine has mostly evaporated, 4 to 6 minutes. Whisk in the blackberries and honey and cook until the berries are soft and falling apart, 5 to 7 minutes. Add the thyme and adjust seasoning.

3. Reduce the heat to low and add the pork chops, overlapping them in the pan. Baste the chops well with the sauce, cover, and cook until warmed through, 1 to 2 minutes. Serve with lemon wedges.

1. Preheat the oven to 350°F. In a small bowl, whisk together the sugar and cornstarch in 2 tablespoons boiling water until dissolved. Whisk in the orange juice and zest.

2. Place the ham steaks in a large baking dish. Pour the glaze over the ham, turning it once to coat it evenly. Bake for 1 hour, flipping the ham occasionally, or until the glaze has thickened and the ham is golden around the edges. Serve hot.

Our Favorite
Hearty Oxtail Stew

Folks, I'm going to tell you a secret now: This here is what I make for Michael when I'm in the mood for love. I swear, as soon as he gets some oxtail in him, he's just as romantic as can be. Don't knock it till you've tried it!

SERVES 4 TO 6

2½ pounds beef oxtails, sliced about 1½ inches thick

1 tablespoon The Lady & Sons House Seasoning (page 66)

4 teaspoons soy sauce

2 large Spanish onions, halved and thinly sliced

2 bay leaves

Cooked white rice, for serving

1. Season the oxtails with the House Seasoning; toss with the soy sauce. Place the oxtails in a slow cooker and add the onions and bay leaves.

2. Cover and cook for 5 to 6 hours on high, until tender. Remove the bay leaves and serve over rice.

Stewed Garlicky Sausage and Peppers

2 large yellow onions, chopped

2 large green bell peppers, seeded and cut into chunks

1 large red bell pepper, seeded and cut into chunks

4 cloves garlic, finely chopped

3 tablespoons extra-virgin olive oil

1¾ pounds sweet or hot Italian sausage, cut into chunks

1 teaspoon dried oregano

Pinch of red pepper flakes

2 tablespoons tomato paste

One 14-ounce can diced tomatoes, undrained

½ cup dry white wine

¼ teaspoon salt

Chopped fresh basil, for garnish

Y ou can put this hearty Italian-style crowd pleaser together so fast you hardly have to think about it. Served with some crusty bread and butter, it's one of my favorite one-pot meals. You know, when a young person asks me for cooking advice, one of the things I like to tell them is to keep sausage (and plenty of bacon) in the freezer. How's that for a golden rule of the kitchen?

(continued)

PAULA'S TIP: **Go ahead and double this pot of deliciousness if you have a crowd coming over, but be sure to double the time in the slow cooker.**

SERVES 4

1. Toss the onions, green and red peppers, and garlic together in a bowl. Heat the oil in a very large skillet over medium-high heat. Add the sausages and brown them, turning occasionally, 7 to 10 minutes. Stir in the oregano and pepper flakes and cook for 30 seconds more. Stir in the tomato paste and cook for another minute. Add the diced tomatoes with their juices, the wine, and salt; simmer for 2 minutes.

2. Arrange half of the onion-and-pepper mixture in the bottom of a slow cooker. Cover with half of the sausages with their sauce, then the rest of the onion-and-pepper mixture. Top with the remaining sausages and sauce. Cover and cook for 4 hours on low or for 2 hours on high. Garnish with basil and serve.

Casseroles and Pasta

If you put it in a pan and you bake it (especially if you've got a little cheese in there), well, then, you've got yourself a casserole. And if you've ever been to a church social, you know there's no limit to what a Southern cook can turn into a casserole. The beauty of these dishes is that you can make them ahead, bring them to wherever you're going, and there you have it, a whole meal in a dish.

Everyone in my family loves to make casseroles for breakfast, lunch, and dinner. When we get together, it's like a casserole convention. And since many of our favorites are baked pastas like lasagna (page 112), or my old-time baked spaghetti (page 108), I figured I'd put all our pasta recipes together with the casseroles. That's also why you'll find Michael's pad thai (page 116) in this chapter, a dish that we used to love ordering at our favorite Thai restaurant, until we realized you could make it even better at home.

Because casseroles are just so comforting and homey and can be made ahead and reheated, and pasta is quick and easy, not to mention delicious, they're both just perfect for everyday meals. Even more than the dessert chapter, these are the recipes I turn to for true ultimate comfort food, whether I'm hankering for Asian flavors or Italian cuisine, or some of that down-home, church social, good ol' Southern cooking. Since these dishes will always please a crowd, feel free to multiply the recipes for your next big family gathering.

Opposite: Cheesy Corn Bread, Spinach, and Turkey Casserole (page 106).

Chicken, Goat Cheese, and Rice Casserole with Pecans and Cherries

Chicken and rice casserole was voted one of my top ten recipes ever by Food Network fans. Well, y'all, here it is all dressed up with goat cheese, pecans, and dried cherries. This is just about the most elegant meal you can serve out of a big ol' casserole dish.

SERVES 6

2 tablespoons (¼ stick) butter

¼ cup chopped yellow onion

1 teaspoon dried thyme

3 cups chicken broth

1½ teaspoons salt

1 teaspoon pepper

2 cups diced cooked chicken

1½ cups long-grain white rice

¾ cup dried cherries

2 cups (½ pound) crumbled goat cheese

1 cup heavy cream

¾ cup chopped pecans

Finely grated zest of 1 orange

1 cup (¼ pound) grated Parmesan cheese

1. Preheat the oven to 375°F. Melt the butter in a medium saucepan. Add the onion and sauté until softened, 5 to 7 minutes. Add the thyme and cook for 1 minute more. Pour in the broth and season with the salt and pepper. Bring the mixture to a boil.

2. In a 13 by 9-inch flameproof baking dish, combine the chicken, rice, and cherries. Pour the boiling broth mixture over it and cover tightly with foil. Bake until the rice is tender and the liquid has been absorbed, 30 to 40 minutes.

3. Remove the casserole from the oven, remove the foil, and turn the setting to broil. Stir in the goat cheese, cream, pecans, and orange zest. Smooth the surface of the casserole and sprinkle it with Parmesan cheese. Return the casserole to the oven and broil until the cheese is melted and golden, about 5 minutes. Serve hot.

3. In a separate bowl, whisk together the corn muffin mix, buttermilk, corn kernels, egg, and ¾ cup of the cheese. Spread the mixture evenly in a thin layer over the turkey mixture. Bake for 10 minutes. Scatter the remaining 1 cup cheese over the top and bake until golden brown, about 20 minutes more. Serve hot.

Four-Cheese and Pesto Italian Baked Spaghetti

If there's one thing better than biting into gooey, bubbling melted cheese, it would be four different cheeses all melted together on top of pesto spaghetti. This is so easy you'll be able to make it almost any night, and once you taste it, that's just what you'll absolutely want to do.

SERVES 6

1 pound uncooked spaghetti

1 pound ricotta cheese

Two 6- to 7-ounce containers prepared pesto

2½ cups (¾ pound) shredded mozzarella

1 cup (¼ pound) grated Parmesan cheese

1 cup (¼ pound) crumbled goat cheese

1. Preheat the oven to 400°F. Grease a flameproof 13 by 9-inch baking dish. Cook the spaghetti for 2 minutes less than the package directions specify. Drain the spaghetti well and transfer it to a bowl. Stir in the ricotta, pesto, 1 cup of the mozzarella, ½ cup of the Parmesan, and the goat cheese. Toss the mixture well and transfer it to the baking dish.

2. Sprinkle the remaining 1½ cups mozzarella and ½ cup Parmesan over the pasta. Bake until the cheese is melted, about 20 minutes. Turn the oven setting to broil and broil for 1 minute or until golden. Serve hot.

Croque-Madame Casserole

I once cooked a Southern meal on TV with a five-star French chef, and, honey, you can believe I just sat back and watched while he went to open a can of biscuits with a can opener. Well, those biscuits blew out of that can and hit him in the face. And naturally, I laughed my butt off. I bet he'd do the same if he heard about my croque-madame casserole. Until he tasted it, that is—then he'd be *begging* me for the recipe! Well, here it is, *monsieur le chef*!

SERVES 6

8 tablespoons (1 stick) butter

¼ cup all-purpose flour

2½ cups milk

2 tablespoons Dijon mustard

¾ teaspoon salt, plus more for seasoning

½ teaspoon pepper, plus more for seasoning

½ teaspoon freshly grated nutmeg

10 to 12 slices white bread

8 ounces (about 8 slices) deli ham

1½ cups (6 ounces) grated Gruyère cheese

6 eggs

1. Preheat the oven to 400°F. Grease an 8-inch square baking dish. To make a béchamel sauce,* melt 6 tablespoons of the butter in a large skillet and cook until bubbling. Whisk in the flour and cook for 1 minute. Slowly whisk in the milk and cook until thick and bubbling, 3 to 5 minutes more. Whisk in the mustard, salt, pepper, and nutmeg.

2. Pour a thin layer of the sauce into the prepared baking dish and cover it with 5 or 6 slices of the bread, then 4 slices of ham and an even layer of the cheese (¾ cup). Repeat the layers once more, ending with a third layer of sauce to cover all. Bake the casserole for 30 minutes. Remove it from the oven and cut it into 6 equal pieces.

3. Fry the eggs. Working in two batches, melt 1 tablespoon of the butter in a large skillet over medium-high heat. Crack 3 eggs into the skillet and season with salt and pepper. Cook until the whites are nearly set, about 3 minutes. Carefully flip the eggs and continue cooking until the whites are completely set, about 1 minute more. You're going to top each portion of the casserole with a fried egg. Repeat with the remaining 3 eggs and 1 tablespoon butter.

* That's just French for a plain ol' white sauce.

Eggplant and Sausage Lasagna

I do love to make lasagna whenever there's a casserole called for, and this recipe is my secret weapon when I'm trying to convince anyone who's on the fence about eggplant. It worked on my boys, and I'm pretty sure it'll work on baby Jack. Go ahead, see if you can't win someone over this way!

SERVES 6

8 ounces uncooked lasagna noodles

½ cup olive oil, plus more for drizzling

1 pound sweet or hot Italian sausage, casings removed, crumbled

One 26-ounce jar pasta sauce

One 15-ounce container ricotta cheese (1½ cups)

1½ cups (6 ounces) grated Parmesan cheese

1 large eggplant (about 1½ pounds), trimmed and cut lengthwise into ½-inch-thick slices

1 teaspoon salt

1 teaspoon pepper

1 pound fresh mozzarella, thinly sliced

2 tablespoons chopped fresh basil, for garnish

1. Cook the pasta in a pot of boiling salted water until al dente, about 8 minutes; drain well. Arrange the noodles in a single layer on a lightly oiled baking sheet. Drizzle the noodles with oil and cover with paper towels.

2. Heat 1 tablespoon of the oil in a large skillet. Add the sausage and brown, breaking it up with a fork, until cooked through, 5 to 7 minutes. Use a slotted spoon to transfer the sausage to a paper towel–lined plate. Drain the excess grease from the skillet. Pour the sauce into the skillet and heat through, scraping up the brown bits of sausage still sticking to the pan. Stir the sausage back into the sauce.

3. Preheat the broiler with the rack 6 inches from the heat source. In a medium bowl, mix the ricotta with 1 cup of the Parmesan. Coat the eggplant slices with the remaining 7 tablespoons of the oil and arrange them in a single layer on a baking sheet; season with the salt and pepper. Broil the slices until tender and golden, turning them once, 3 to 4 minutes per side.

4. Reduce the oven temperature to 375°F. In a lightly greased 13 by 9-inch baking dish, layer one third of the sauce,

half of the noodles, half of the eggplant slices, half of the ricotta mixture, and half of the mozzarella slices. Repeat, ending with a final layer of pasta sauce. Top with the remaining ½ cup Parmesan. Bake until golden and bubbling, about 40 minutes. Sprinkle with the basil before serving.

Smoky Tomato-Bacon Pasta

I cannot imagine a life, or even a week, without bacon and pasta (or macaroni, as we always called it when I was growing up), so it was just a matter of time before I got around to putting the two together. When I did, well, I've been trying to watch my language since my grandbaby, Jack, was born, so all I can say is, holy crumb, that's my kind of pasta: creamy, smoky, and zesty. You won't be able to resist.

SERVES 4 TO 6

½ pound bacon (about 10 slices)

1 large yellow onion, chopped

One 28-ounce can diced tomatoes, undrained

Salt and pepper

4 ounces cream cheese (half of an 8-ounce package), cut into pieces

1 pound uncooked rigatoni

1. In a large skillet, cook the bacon until crisp and brown. Transfer it to a paper towel–lined plate. Pour off all but ¼ cup fat from the skillet.

2. Add the onion and cook over medium heat, stirring occasionally, until softened, 5 to 7 minutes. Stir in the diced tomatoes, then crumble in the bacon. Season with salt and pepper; simmer, stirring occasionally, until thick and chunky, about 10 minutes. Stir in the cream cheese until melted.

3. Meanwhile, in a large pot of boiling salted water, cook the rigatoni according to the package directions. Drain and transfer to a large bowl. Toss with the sauce and serve immediately.

Bubba's Creamy, Spicy Seafood Pasta

2 tablespoons olive oil

2 cloves garlic, minced

½ cup vodka

One 14-ounce can crushed tomatoes

½ cup heavy cream

½ teaspoon red pepper flakes, or to taste

Salt and pepper

½ pound bay scallops

½ pound large shrimp, peeled, deveined, and cut crosswise into thirds

1 pound uncooked linguine

I love vodka sauce—it's got cream, garlic, and tomatoes in it. How can you go wrong? So when Bubba first served me his seafood pasta, I saw just where he was coming from. And I wasn't surprised to see that he'd loaded it up with seafood. He loves going fishing and crabbing and he never misses an opportunity to add the day's catch to his cooking.

BUBBA SAYS: **Every now and then I like to switch things up and have folks over for a pasta supper, and I love any kind of pasta that's got some kick to it. Make sure to have yourself some bread with this meal to soak up every bit of that good, spicy sauce. You know I never forget to have the bread, and it shows!**

SERVES 2 TO 4

1. Heat the oil in a large skillet over medium heat. Add the garlic and cook for 1 minute or until fragrant. Add the vodka and turn the heat up to medium-high; cook until the liquid has reduced by half. Add the tomatoes, cream, pepper flakes, and salt and pepper to taste. Cook, stirring occasionally, for 3 to 5 minutes, until thickened. Add the seafood and cook for about 3 minutes, until it's just opaque.

2. Meanwhile, cook the pasta in a large pot of boiling salted water according to the package directions. Drain and transfer the pasta to a large bowl, pour the sauce over it, and toss to combine. Serve immediately.

Michael's Better-Than-Takeout Pad Thai

We have such an excellent Thai restaurant nearby, and we just love to get take-out for a change of pace. Michael got hooked on pad thai years ago, and after ordering it in for the billionth time, he up and made his own one night. Bless him, he can cook even better than he lets on.

PAULA'S TIP: **To get every last tasty ingredient cooked at the right time, it's easiest to just make this recipe in two batches. But don't worry about the first batch getting cold while you do the second; the cooking goes quick.**

SERVES 4 TO 6

1. Soak the noodles in a bowl of warm water until softened, about 10 minutes; drain.

2. Whisk together the ½ cup oil with the brown sugar, fish sauce, vinegar, lime juice, and tamarind concentrate. Heat the mixture in a medium saucepan until the sugar dissolves, about 5 minutes. Keep warm.

3. Heat the 3 tablespoons oil in a large wok or skillet (or do this in two batches in a smaller pan). Add the sliced green onions, garlic, and jalapeño; cook for 1 minute. Add the noodles and half of the sauce; cook for 5 minutes. Push the noodles to the side of the wok and crack the eggs into the center. Let cook for 15 seconds before tossing the eggs into the noodles. Once again, push the noodles to the side of the pan. Add the shrimp, tomatoes, 1½ cups of the bean sprouts, and

Two 8-ounce packages pad thai rice noodles

½ cup plus 3 tablespoons peanut or vegetable oil

½ cup packed light brown sugar

3 tablespoons Asian fish sauce

1½ tablespoons sherry vinegar

1½ tablespoons freshly squeezed lime juice

1½ teaspoons tamarind concentrate (see Note)

½ cup thinly sliced green onions (scallions), white and light green parts; chop the dark green parts for garnish

2 cloves garlic, finely chopped

1 jalapeño pepper, seeded if desired and finely chopped

3 eggs

1 pound large shrimp, peeled and deveined

2 medium tomatoes, cut into wedges

2 cups bean sprouts, drained

1¼ cups chopped peanuts, roasted or raw

⅓ cup chopped cilantro, for garnish

¾ cup of the peanuts. Stir-fry until the shrimp are cooked through, about 5 minutes, then add the remaining sauce and toss everything together with the noodles. Garnish with the remaining ½ cup bean sprouts and ½ cup peanuts, the chopped green onions, and the cilantro. Serve immediately.

NOTE: Tamarind concentrate, also sold as tamarind paste, is an extremely tart flavoring with a citrusy tang made from the podlike fruit of the tamarind tree. It's commonly used in Southeast Asian cooking, but is becoming more and more popular here in the West. You can find it in the international section of large supermarkets.

Asparagus Risotto with Shrimp and Scallops

This dish is so creamy and buttery, which is just about the only way I can get my man to eat his vegetables. The seafood makes it special enough for company, too, so serve it to friends when you want to knock their socks off. I can guarantee the results!

SERVES 4 TO 6

8 cups chicken broth

5 tablespoons butter

2 cups Arborio rice (see Note)

1 teaspoon salt

1 cup dry white wine

1 cup frozen peas, thawed

½ pound large shrimp, peeled, deveined, and cut crosswise into thirds

½ pound sea scallops, quartered

½ pound asparagus, trimmed and cut into 1-inch pieces

1 tablespoon chopped fresh chives

Finely grated zest of 1 lemon

Pepper

Grated Parmesan cheese, for serving

1. In a medium saucepan, bring the broth to a simmer and keep it warm over low heat.

2. Melt the butter in a large skillet over medium heat. Add the rice and salt; cook until the rice is translucent, stirring with a wooden spoon to coat the grains, about 3 minutes. Add the wine and cook until it has mostly evaporated, about 2 minutes. Ladle 1 cup of the hot broth into the rice and stir until it's absorbed. Add more broth, 1 cup at a time, until the rice can no longer absorb liquid; there should be at least 2 cups of broth remaining in the saucepan.

3. Let the rice rest, covered and off the heat, for 10 to 15 minutes. The rice should be creamy, but still have some bite to it. Stir in the peas.

4. Return the remaining broth to a simmer. Add the shrimp, scallops, and asparagus to the broth; simmer until the seafood is just opaque, about 2 minutes. Using a slotted spoon, transfer the shrimp, scallops, and asparagus to the risotto and stir well to combine. Stir in the chives and lemon zest; season with pepper. Serve the risotto hot, topped with grated Parmesan.

NOTE: Arborio rice is a short-grain, pearl-like rice commonly used in Italian-style dishes. It has a higher starch content than other varieties of white rice, which gives it a creamier texture when cooked. Arborio rice is available in better supermarkets everywhere.

3. Melt the butter in a large skillet over medium-high heat. Add the onion and green pepper and cook for 5 minutes or until tender. Add the mirliton pulp and cook for 5 minutes more. Add the shrimp and sausage and cook until the shrimp are just opaque, about 4 minutes. Stir in the bread crumbs, seasoning, and salt.

4. Stuff the mirliton shells with the filling. Place the stuffed mirlitons on a baking sheet and bake for 35 to 45 minutes, until the tops are golden brown. Serve hot.

Good Food That's Good for You (or, Recipes for a Later Age)

These days, whenever I have the chance, I try to make the right choices about what I eat, because if we all live long enough, there's a good chance that we're going to be at risk for high cholesterol, type 2 diabetes, or high blood pressure. As we grow older, we have to use moderation a little more than we did when we were younger. So as much as I love fried chicken and biscuits and gravy, I know that I can't in good faith let myself go down that path every day.

You know me, though; I'm not one to sit around nibbling on carrots. The recipes in this chapter will suit anyone who has to modify their diet, but they're still chock-full of all the big, bold flavors that I love. So how do I manage to make them on the lighter side? Well, I take advantage of all the fresh, beautiful seafood I can get in Savannah, and the great produce. And all my favorite seasonings—

Opposite: Oven-Fried Chicken Breasts with Honey-Yogurt Drizzle (page 158) and Corn and Carrot Slaw with Golden Raisins (page 148).

garlic, chile peppers, curry powder, hot sauce, and vinegar—fit right in with those healthful ingredients.

And I've got to hand it to my handsome son Bobby. When it comes to healthful cooking, he really leads the way in our family, coming up with delicious new ways to turn fish and veggies into a feast. It's wonderful when you can learn so much from your children, and when it comes to cooking healthful meals for Michael and me to enjoy, I've got plenty of incentive: I plan to be around to make baby Jack as many big sugar-and-butter-filled birthday cakes as I can.

Jack's already following in his daddy Jamie's footsteps; you gotta start 'em cookin' while they're young!

Red Pepper–Balsamic Dip

DIP

1 cup chopped roasted red bell peppers

One 8-ounce package Neufchâtel cheese

¼ cup light mayonnaise

¼ cup fresh basil leaves

2 green onions (scallions), white and light green parts, trimmed and cut into chunks

1 clove garlic, roughly chopped

Finely grated zest of 1 lemon

¼ teaspoon salt

¼ teaspoon pepper

Pita chips

Raw vegetables such as carrot or celery sticks or radishes

I could eat chips and sour cream dip until the cows come home, but I wouldn't call that the healthiest snack in the world. So when I'm feeling like being moderate, I'll whip up a lighter dip like this one, which is still delicious and tangy-sweet even if it is pretty good for you. Serve it with baked chips or a mountain of cut-up veggies; I promise, it'll perk up whatever you've got. And if you serve it at a party, don't tell anyone it's on the lighter side; it's tasty enough so no one will notice.

MAKES ABOUT 2 CUPS

Combine all the ingredients for the dip in a food processor and pulse until smooth. Serve with pita chips or raw vegetables.

Corn and Carrot Slaw with Golden Raisins

Carrot slaw is so easy to make, and the sweet crunch goes especially well with grilled chicken or meat. I like to fix this when Michael's cooking in the outdoor kitchen, or bring it to a potluck, where it holds up great all day long.

SERVES 4 (SMALL SERVINGS)

1. In a small bowl, whisk together the mayonnaise, oil, and lemon juice.

2. In a large bowl, combine the carrots, corn kernels, raisins, and parsley. Pour the dressing over the salad and season with salt and pepper. Serve immediately or store, covered, in the refrigerator.

2 tablespoons light mayonnaise

1 tablespoon extra virgin olive oil

1 tablespoon freshly squeezed lemon juice

½ pound carrots, grated (2 cups)

1 cup frozen corn kernels, thawed and drained

½ cup golden raisins

5 tablespoons chopped fresh parsley

Salt and pepper

Light and Lemony English Pea Salad

½ cup light mayonnaise

2 tablespoons freshly squeezed lemon juice

2 teaspoons finely grated lemon zest

2 tablespoons chopped fresh chives

Two 10-ounce packages frozen peas, thawed and drained

Salt

This is a gorgeous summertime salad that should be served and savored in a pretty bowl.

SERVES 2 TO 4

In a small bowl, mix the mayonnaise, lemon juice and zest, and chives. Pour over the peas, toss to coat, and season to taste with salt.

Fresh Fruit Ambrosia

Your mouth might call this dessert, but where I'm from, it's a salad. I grew up just loving anything with marshmallows in it, and this light, juicy recipe was always a hit at family picnics.

PAULA'S TIP: **For a toasted marshmallow variation, layer the ingredients as directed in a flameproof baking dish. Place the dish under the broiler until the marshmallows are golden and puffed, 1 to 2 minutes (watch carefully that they don't burn).**

SERVES 4 TO 6

6 navel oranges (about 4½ pounds)

1 cup mini marshmallows

¾ cup sweetened flaked coconut

½ cup (3 ounces) diced dried pineapple

Confectioners' sugar, for serving

1. Cut off the tops and bottoms of the oranges, just exposing the flesh. With a sharp knife, cut the peel away, following the curve of the fruit and completely removing the white pith. Cut out the sections of the oranges, cutting in along the membrane, and reserve the juice.

2. Arrange the orange sections on a platter. Sprinkle them evenly with the marshmallows, coconut, and pineapple. Drizzle with the reserved orange juice and dust with confectioners' sugar.

Quick Curried Zucchini-Apple Soup with Toasted Almonds

This soup is so light and elegant, I make it for company when I want to be sure we'll have room for the main course. You can also serve it with some nice crusty bread and a big salad for a lunch that won't slow you down.

SERVES 4

2 teaspoons olive oil, preferably extra-virgin

1 medium yellow onion, finely chopped

1 clove garlic, minced

2 teaspoons curry powder

¾ teaspoon ground cumin

Pinch of cayenne pepper

4 medium zucchini (1½ pounds), trimmed and cut into chunks

1 quart chicken broth

1 medium Granny Smith apple, peeled, cored, and chopped (about 1 cup)

¾ teaspoon salt

¾ teaspoon pepper

¼ cup toasted sliced almonds, for garnish

Brooke's got Jack eatin' healthy.

1. Heat the oil in a medium pot over medium-high heat. Add the onion and garlic and cook until softened, about 5 minutes. Stir in the curry powder, cumin, and cayenne; cook for 1 minute. Add the zucchini and chicken broth; simmer for 10 minutes. Stir in the apple and simmer until tender, about 5 minutes. Season with the salt and pepper.

2. Carefully transfer the soup to a blender and puree it in batches until smooth. Reheat, ladle it into soup bowls, and serve, garnished with the toasted almonds.

Easy Poached Salmon with Lemon and Herbs

Does cooking get any easier or healthier than poaching a nice big piece of fresh salmon? I'll fix this for lunch on days when it's just Michael and me at the table, or I'll scale it up for a festive occasion. And on hot summer days, I love to chill the salmon and serve it with a nice dollop of mustard mixed with light mayonnaise.

SERVES 4

1 cup dry white wine

4 green onions (scallions), white and light green parts, trimmed and cut into 2-inch lengths

Salt

2 bay leaves

Four 8-ounce skinless salmon fillets

Pepper

8 sprigs fresh rosemary

1 lemon, thinly sliced into rounds

1. In a large skillet, simmer 3 cups water with the wine, green onions, 2 teaspoons salt, and the bay leaves for 5 minutes.

2. Lightly season the salmon with salt and pepper and top each fillet with 2 rosemary sprigs and a lemon slice. Place the salmon in the skillet over medium heat, adding additional water if needed to reach about two thirds of the way up the fillets. Cover the skillet and simmer until just cooked through, about 8 minutes per inch of thickness. Transfer the salmon fillets to plates, discard the bay leaves, and drizzle the pan juices over them for serving.

Parmesan Tilapia Roll-Ups

½ cup light mayonnaise

½ cup (2 ounces) grated
Parmesan cheese

¼ cup chopped fresh parsley

2 cloves garlic, finely chopped

Eight 3- to 4-ounce tilapia fillets

Salt and pepper

Extra-virgin olive oil

Lemon wedges, for serving

A mild, light-tasting white fish like tilapia is perfect for a healthy supper, especially when dressed up with some grated Parmesan cheese.

PAULA'S TIP: **You don't want to use too much Parmesan cheese here; the flavor of the fish really should be the star.**

SERVES 4

1. Preheat the oven to 375°F. In a bowl, stir together the mayonnaise, cheese, parsley, and garlic.

2. Season the fillets on both sides with salt and pepper. Spread the tops with the mayonnaise mixture. Roll up the fillets to cover the filling, and secure each with several toothpicks. Brush the outsides lightly with oil. Arrange the roll-ups on a baking sheet. Bake until the fish is opaque and just cooked through, 10 to 15 minutes. Serve with lemon wedges.

Seared Scallops with Pineapple-Cucumber Salsa

Searing scallops is one of the fastest dishes I know, and you know I put a premium on recipes I can whip up in no time flat, especially when Michael and I want to have a romantic dinner by ourselves. On nights like those, the last thing I want is to spend the whole evening in the kitchen! I also adore the salsa on fish or grilled chicken.

SERVES 4

1. In a bowl, combine the cucumber, pineapple, cilantro, red onion, lime zest, jalapeño, salt, and hot sauce. Taste and adjust the seasoning, if necessary.

2. Rinse the scallops and pat them very dry, then season them with salt and pepper.

3. Warm the oil in a large skillet over medium-high heat. Sear the scallops, without moving them in the pan, until golden, 2 to 3 minutes per side. Serve with a generous topping of salsa.

SALSA

1 cup diced peeled cucumber (about 1 medium cucumber)

1 cup canned diced pineapple, drained

3 tablespoons chopped cilantro

1 tablespoon finely chopped red onion

2½ teaspoons finely grated lime zest

2 teaspoons finely chopped jalapeño pepper

¼ teaspoon salt, plus more to taste

¼ teaspoon Paula Deen Hot Sauce or other hot sauce

SCALLOPS

2 pounds sea scallops

Salt and pepper

2½ tablespoons olive oil

Oven-Fried Chicken Breasts with Honey-Yogurt Drizzle

I have to work around my love for fried chicken if I am going to eat well, so I came up with this tasty oven-fried variation. It satisfies the itch, and with the yogurt and honey sauce, your kids will love it, too.

SERVES 4

2½ cups cornflakes

2½ teaspoons The Lady & Sons House Seasoning (page 66)

½ cup buttermilk

Four 8-ounce boneless, skinless chicken breast halves

½ cup plain low-fat yogurt

2 tablespoons honey

1. Preheat the oven to 350°F. Spray a baking sheet with nonstick cooking spray. Put the cornflakes in a gallon-size heavy-duty plastic bag and crush them (a rolling pin is good for this). Add 2 teaspoons of the House Seasoning, shake to combine, and pour onto a plate. Pour the buttermilk into a shallow bowl.

2. Pat the chicken dry and sprinkle it with the remaining ½ teaspoon seasoning. Dip each breast into the buttermilk and then into the crushed cornflakes, pressing the flakes to help them adhere. Transfer the chicken breasts to the prepared baking sheet and bake until golden and cooked through, 25 to 30 minutes.

3. While the chicken is baking, in a small bowl, mix together the yogurt and honey. Serve the sauce alongside the chicken.

Spicy Chicken and Green Chile Chili

3 tablespoons olive oil

1 medium yellow onion, finely chopped

1½ teaspoons ground cumin

2 pounds ground chicken

One 16-ounce jar salsa verde

2 cups chicken broth

1 green bell pepper, seeded and finely diced

One 4-ounce can chopped green chiles

2 fat cloves garlic, finely chopped

1½ cups baked tortilla chips (about 2 ounces)

⅓ cup chopped cilantro

1 teaspoon salt

½ teaspoon pepper

Light or nonfat sour cream, or serving

The good fiery flavor of green chile adds a lot of oomph to my healthiest chili recipe. It's great with a dollop of light or nonfat sour cream on top.

SERVES 4 TO 6

1. Warm the oil in a large skillet over medium-high heat. Add the onion and sauté until softened, about 5 minutes. Add the cumin and cook for 1 minute more. Add the chicken and cook, breaking it up with a fork, until brown, about 10 minutes.

2. Transfer the mixture to a slow cooker. Add the salsa, broth, green pepper, chiles, and garlic and cook for 3 hours on high or for 7 hours on low; then uncover and continue cooking for another hour.

3. Add the tortilla chips and cook uncovered for 15 minutes more. Stir in the cilantro, salt, and pepper and spoon into bowls. Serve topped with sour cream.

Grilled Orange-Glazed Pork Tenderloin

For her dinners with her seven best girlfriends, Aunt Peggy always makes her Orange-Glazed Ham Steak (page 94) that's just to die for. It is so good I wake up in the middle of the night thinking about it. So one day I created my own version using grilled pork tenderloin, which is very lean, glazed with orange juice but no sugar. It's perfect when I want that fruity, meaty flavor with a lighter touch.

SERVES 4 TO 6

1 cup orange juice

¼ cup olive oil

2 cloves garlic, chopped

1 teaspoon salt

Two 1¼-pound pork tenderloins

⅓ cup honey

Vegetable oil, for brushing the grill

1. In a blender, combine the orange juice, olive oil, garlic, and salt, and blend until smooth. Place the tenderloins in a 2.5-gallon resealable plastic bag or a large bowl. Pour the marinade over them, seal or cover with plastic wrap, and marinate in the refrigerator for 8 hours or overnight.

2. Fire up the grill. Remove the tenderloins from the marinade and pat dry. Pour the marinade into a small saucepan, add the honey, and let the mixture boil until it is reduced to a syrupy consistency, about 20 minutes.

3. Meanwhile, brush the grill with oil and grill the pork over medium heat for 20 minutes, turning occasionally. Brush some of the orange glaze over the pork and continue to cook, brushing with more glaze, until an internal temperature of 150°F is reached (check with an instant-read thermometer), about 20 minutes more. Let the pork rest for a few minutes before slicing.

Grilled Beef Tenderloin and Vidalia Onion Skewers

1/3 cup apple cider vinegar

8 cloves garlic, minced

2 teaspoons grated Parmesan cheese

2 teaspoons freshly squeezed lemon juice

1 teaspoon paprika

1 teaspoon sugar

1 teaspoon The Lady & Sons House Seasoning (page 66)

1/2 teaspoon dried oregano

2 pounds beef tenderloin, trimmed and cut into 2-inch cubes

4 tablespoons (1/2 stick) butter, melted

1 beef bouillon cube, crushed

4 large Vidalia onions, cut into 2-inch cubes

This is my kind of healthful recipe: the kind you'd make whether you intended to be healthful or not. The lean but juicy marinated meat goes so nicely with the sweetness of the grilled onions that there's no need to pile on extra sauce. Michael makes these all summer long and we never get tired of this simple meal.

SERVES 6 TO 8

1. In a shallow dish, whisk together the vinegar, garlic, Parmesan, lemon juice, paprika, sugar, House Seasoning, and oregano. Add the beef cubes and marinate, covered, for 1 hour.

2. Light the grill or preheat the broiler. In a bowl, combine the melted butter and bouillon, until the bouillon is completely dissolved.

3. Using metal or soaked bamboo skewers, skewer the beef and onion cubes separately. Brush the onions with the butter mixture. Place the skewers on the grill or, if broiling, transfer the skewers to a foil-lined baking sheet and broil. Turn once, until the onion is tender and the beef is cooked to the desired doneness, 3 to 5 minutes per side.

Breakfast and Brunch

I will admit, I have been known to skip breakfast when things get busy, but on the weekends, holidays (especially Christmas morning, when I go all out), and anytime I've got family around, there's nothing I love better than cooking up a real morning meal. Breakfast time is such a great way to get together, since you can include the kids. And I love to have fun with my breakfast menus, dressing up the old favorites like waffles, pancakes, eggs, and French toast. What better way is there to start off a Sunday than with a big ol' platter of Cornmeal Biscuits with Blackberry Butter (page 180) or a hearty Breakfast Strata with Mushrooms, Shrimp, and Brie (page 166), and a table full of your nearest and dearest to share them with?

My boys have always been able to put away some serious breakfast, and when they were growing, I found I had to stuff them full of protein first thing, or they'd be back in the kitchen begging for something to tide them over an hour later. We've come up with some hearty dishes for breakfast and brunch over the years, and I never like to leave out the sweet side—the pancakes and the baking. That's got to be my favorite thing about brunch—you can mix the sweet stuff and the savory to your heart's delight.

Opposite: Jamie's Huevos Rancheros (page 165).

What a treat it is to have a warm, just-made muffin or a piece of coffee cake with your coffee! But I always take a few shortcuts when I can in the morning. Sure, you want those breakfast treats freshly made, but you don't want to be getting up with the roosters just to get them in the oven. You won't be able to taste that I've used a few little time-savers, but you'll sure appreciate them when that alarm goes off.

Bobby Deen never met a breakfast he didn't like.

Jamie's Huevos Rancheros

One 15-ounce can whole peeled tomatoes, undrained

¼ cup diced yellow onion

¼ cup cilantro leaves, plus more for garnish

1 large clove garlic

1 jalapeño pepper (seeded if desired)

½ teaspoon salt

5 ounces chorizo, casings removed, diced

Vegetable oil

Four 6-inch corn tortillas, plus more for serving (optional)

One 16-ounce can refried beans (optional)

8 eggs

1 avocado, pitted, peeled, and diced

¾ cup (3 ounces) crumbled queso fresco or grated Monterey Jack, for serving

Sour cream, for serving

Since baby Jack came along, Jamie and Brooke have found themselves making less of a fuss about dinner because they're just dog tired by the time Jack's in bed. The trade-off is that they make some real special breakfasts for each other. Jamie cooks these Mexican-style eggs for us all at brunch, too.

SERVES 4

1. In a food processor, combine the tomatoes (with juices), onion, cilantro, garlic, jalapeño, and ½ teaspoon salt; puree until smooth. Transfer the mixture to a small skillet and simmer over medium heat until slightly thickened, about 10 minutes. Cover and keep warm over low heat.

2. In a large skillet over medium-high heat, cook the chorizo until browned. Add to the sauce and cover again.

3. Add 1 tablespoon vegetable oil to the fat in the large skillet. Place a tortilla in the skillet and cook until light golden but not crisp, about 30 seconds. Flip and cook for 30 seconds more. Transfer to an individual plate. Cook the remaining tortillas, adding a bit more oil to the pan, if necessary.

4. Heat the refried beans (if using) in the large skillet. Spread the beans on the tortillas.

5. Add another tablespoon of oil to the skillet. Working in batches, crack the eggs into the pan. Cook until the bottoms are set and the edges are golden, 1 to 2 minutes. Turn the heat to medium-low, cover, and cook until set, about 1 minute more. Place 2 eggs on each tortilla and spoon the warm sauce over the eggs. Sprinkle with the avocado, cheese, and additional cilantro. Top with a dollop of sour cream.

Breakfast Strata with Mushrooms, Shrimp, and Brie

This is just the thing for when you have the whole family over for brunch. You have to put it together an hour before you bake it, so I make it first thing, then I have something light to tide me over while we're waiting for everyone to show up! Or you could assemble this the night before, then bake it in the morning. Just be sure to serve it hot from the oven when the cheese is at its gooey melted best.

SERVES 6 TO 8

3 tablespoons butter

1/3 cup chopped green onions (scallions), white and light green parts

1 teaspoon dried thyme

2½ cups (8 ounces) sliced white mushrooms

1 pound large shrimp, peeled and deveined

1¼ teaspoons salt

¾ teaspoon pepper

One 16- to 20-inch loaf French bread, cut into 2-inch cubes (about 8 cups)

½ pound Brie cheese, rind removed, cut into pieces

8 eggs

2 cups milk

1. Grease a 13 by 9-inch baking dish. Melt 2 tablespoons of the butter in a large skillet over medium-high heat. Sauté the green onions until softened, about 2 minutes. Add the thyme and cook for another 30 seconds. Add the mushrooms and cook until softened, about 5 minutes.

2. Move the mushrooms and green onions to one side of the pan and place the remaining 1 tablespoon butter on the empty side. Add the shrimp and cook, stirring constantly, until just opaque, about 2 minutes. Toss the shrimp and mushroom mixture together; season with ½ teaspoon each of the salt and pepper. Remove the pan from the heat and transfer the mixture to a bowl.

3. Place the bread cubes and cheese in the baking dish. Scatter the shrimp-mushroom mixture over the bread and the Brie.

4. In a bowl, whisk together the eggs, milk, and the remaining ¾ teaspoon salt and ¼ teaspoon pepper. Pour the custard

over the bread, pressing the mixture down to soak the cubes. Cover the strata and let stand for at least 1 hour or up to overnight in the refrigerator.

5. Preheat the oven to 350°F. Bake the strata until golden and the custard is set, about 50 minutes. Serve immediately.

Bobby's Whole Wheat and Honey Pancakes

These are just like my Bobby, wholesome and hearty and more than a little bit sweet.

MAKES 16 PANCAKES, TO SERVE 4

1. To make the honey butter, whisk the butter, honey, and lime zest in a bowl until smooth, or pulse to combine them in a mini food processor.

2. To make the pancakes, whisk together the flours, baking soda, salt, and cinnamon in a bowl. In a separate bowl, whisk together the buttermilk, eggs, melted butter, and honey. Stir the wet ingredients into the dry ones until just combined; don't worry about lumps.

3. Melt 1 tablespoon of butter in a large skillet over medium-high heat. Working in batches, drop the batter, about ¼ cup at a time, into the skillet. Cook until the surface is bubbling and the bottom is golden brown, 2 to 3 minutes. Flip each pancake and cook until the bottom is golden brown and the pancake is firm, about 2 minutes more. Cover the pancakes with foil and repeat with the remaining batter, using more butter if necessary. Serve topped with the honey butter.

HONEY BUTTER

4 tablespoons (½ stick) butter, softened

¼ cup honey

Finely grated zest of 1 lime

PANCAKES

1½ cups all-purpose flour

½ cup whole wheat flour

½ teaspoon baking soda

½ teaspoon salt

¼ teaspoon ground cinnamon

2 cups buttermilk

2 eggs

4 tablespoons (½ stick) butter, melted, plus more for cooking

1 tablespoon honey

Katie Lee Joel's Pumpkin Soufflé Pancake

I just love Katie Lee Joel. I met her a few years back at the South Beach Wine & Food Festival. I had gotten word that Katie was a big fan, and that she and her husband, Billy Joel, were going to be bringing their boat up the coast. So she and Billy stopped in and we spent a couple of hours together and just had the best time. Billy's this great down-to-earth guy and Katie's a precious young woman. She's so smart and beautiful, and so sweet.

After they left, Michael said, "Oh, what a nice couple. Bill and I have a lot in common." And I said, "You do?" He said, "Yeah, we both married Southern girls, we both love boats and motorcycles, and we both play instruments." "You play what?" I asked, figuring he'd been holding out on me. "He plays the piano and I play the radio." We've all been fast friends ever since.

Here's Katie's recipe for a fluffy, sweet baked pancake filled with pumpkin and nuts. She made it on my show a while back and I've been dreaming about it ever since. Luckily I can just wake up and throw it together for breakfast. Don't you love it when dreams come true?

SERVES 4 TO 6

4 tablespoons (½ stick) butter

1 tablespoon packed light brown sugar

¼ cup pecan halves

4 eggs, separated

⅔ cup buttermilk

1¼ teaspoons vanilla extract

⅔ cup all-purpose flour

1 teaspoon pumpkin pie spice

¼ teaspoon salt

1 cup pumpkin puree

⅓ cup granulated sugar

Confectioners' sugar, for dusting

Maple syrup, for serving

1. Preheat the oven to 375°F. Melt the butter in a large ovenproof skillet over medium-low heat. Transfer 3 tablespoons of the butter to a medium bowl. Add the brown sugar to the remaining butter in the skillet and stir until the sugar begins to melt, 2 to 3 minutes. Add the pecans and cook for 2 minutes more. Transfer the pecan mixture to a small dish and set aside. Keep the skillet for cooking the pancake.

2. Add the egg yolks, buttermilk, and vanilla to the bowl with the melted butter and whisk to blend. In a separate bowl, mix together the flour, pumpkin pie spice, and salt. Gradually whisk the flour mixture into the egg yolk mixture; stir in the pumpkin puree and set aside.

3. Whip the egg whites until frothy, gradually add the granulated sugar, and beat until stiff peaks form. Gently fold the egg whites into the pumpkin mixture. Pour the batter into the skillet and sprinkle the top of the pancake with the pecan mixture.

4. Bake for 25 to 30 minutes, until golden brown. Dust the top of the pancake with the confectioners' sugar, cut into wedges, and serve hot with maple syrup.

T.J.'s Cream Cheese and Strawberry–Stuffed French Toast

2 eggs

½ cup milk

½ teaspoon granulated sugar

4 ounces cream cheese (half of an 8-ounce package)

12 slices white bread

1 cup sliced fresh strawberries

Butter, for cooking

Maple syrup or confectioners' sugar, for serving

T.J. is Kelley and George's son, and even as a high school student, he already loves to cook—at least when it comes to making this scrumptious cream cheese–stuffed French toast.

KELLEY SAYS: This idea came home with T.J. from a high school communications class where students were asked to give a demonstration speech. T.J. loves it so much that he frequently makes it for himself and anyone else who is around for a lazy weekend breakfast.

MAKES 6 SANDWICHES, TO SERVE 4 TO 6

1. In a small bowl, whisk together the eggs, milk, and granulated sugar. Spread the cream cheese on 6 slices of the bread. Divide the strawberries among the 6 bread slices. Top with the remaining 6 slices and press around the edges to seal.

2. Melt butter on a griddle over medium-low heat. Dip the sandwiches in the egg mixture for a few seconds on each side. Cook the sandwiches until golden brown, 2 to 3 minutes per side. Serve with maple syrup or confectioners' sugar.

Bananas Foster French Toast

When my boys were little, we had this pit bull named Blue who was the most snuggly and lovable old fella you'd ever want to meet. Well, I remember one day I was yelling at those two slug-a-bed sons of mine to get up and go help their daddy with the yard work. And don't you know old Blue put his head up from under the covers and growled a low mean growl that told me that nobody was ready to get up yet. I said, "Screw it, y'all can sleep in. You, too, Blue." And I got going on breakfast. Those boys of mine ate well, all right. Here's my latest variation on French toast; it smells so good frying up nobody needs an alarm clock to show up at the breakfast table.

SERVES 4 TO 6

4 eggs

1 cup heavy cream

1 teaspoon ground cinnamon

4 tablespoons (½ stick) butter

8 large croissants, sliced in half

1 cup maple syrup

½ cup dark corn syrup

½ cup packed brown sugar

6 ripe bananas, halved crosswise
   and then lengthwise

1 cup chopped pecans

1 teaspoon rum extract

1. In a small bowl, whisk together the eggs, cream, and cinnamon.

2. Melt 2 tablespoons of the butter in a large skillet over medium-high heat. Coat 4 of the croissant halves in the egg mixture, allowing the excess to drip back into the bowl. Place the croissant halves in the skillet and cook for 2 to 3 minutes per side, until lightly browned. Transfer them to a plate and cover with foil to keep warm. Repeat, using the remaining croissant halves and butter.

3. Add the maple syrup, corn syrup, and brown sugar to the skillet. Bring to a boil, stirring, over medium-high heat. Reduce the heat to medium-low and simmer for 2 minutes. Add the banana quarters, turning to coat with the syrup, and the pecans, and simmer for 1 minute. Stir in the rum extract. Spoon the sauce over the croissants and serve immediately.

Kelley's Oatmeal and Currant Scones

These fabulous scones are sweet and hearty. I do not see the point of a dry scone, and Kelley's are moist and very tender—and even better with some butter and jam on top.

KELLEY SAYS: **These are wonderful when served as a snack with a morning cup of coffee or tea, or as part of a big brunch.**

MAKES 8 SCONES

1¼ cups all-purpose flour, plus more for kneading

¼ cup sugar

2 teaspoons baking powder

½ teaspoon salt

4 tablespoons (½ stick) butter, chilled and cubed

½ cup quick-cooking oats

¼ cup dried currants

½ cup heavy cream

1. Preheat the oven to 425°F. Lightly grease a baking sheet. In a small bowl or a food processor, combine the flour, sugar, baking powder, and salt. Cut the butter into the mixture using a pastry cutter or fork, or pulse it in the food processor, until it resembles coarse meal. Stir in the oats and currants. Mix in the heavy cream until the mixture forms big crumbs.

2. On a lightly floured surface, gently knead until the mixture comes together in a ball, about 30 seconds. Pat it into a round about 9 inches in diameter and roughly 2 inches thick. Cut the round into quarters, then cut each quarter in half to form wedges.

3. Place the wedges on the prepared baking sheet and bake until the bottoms are lightly browned, about 22 minutes. Transfer to a rack for cooling.

Mama's Old-Fashioned White Bread

STARTER

One ¼-ounce package active dry yeast (2¼ teaspoons)

½ cup instant mashed potato flakes

½ cup sugar

2 teaspoons salt

BREAD

1 cup starter

6 cups bread flour, plus more as needed

½ cup corn oil, plus more for brushing

½ cup sugar

1 tablespoon salt

This is my Grandmama Irene Paul's bread, and it is certainly one of our most cherished family recipes. My cousin Dion (Aunt Trina's daughter) sent it along when she heard I was working on this book. I hadn't had it in years, and was so happy to bite into a soft, tangy slice. It was a taste of my childhood, that's for sure!

The original recipe says to give the dough two rises of 6 to 8 hours each, but you may find your bread may need as little as half that time, 3 to 4 hours each rise.

DION SAYS: **Every one of us knew that anytime we went to Nana's, there would always be loaves of her homemade yeast bread. As kids, our favorite was the cinnamon-raisin bread— with icing, of course! My mama recently found Nana's basic bread recipe for me, and I went right out and started making it. I soon filled my freezer and my daughter's freezer with homemade bread. There is nothing like the smell of fresh bread baking! I hope that my daughter will one day start baking it, too, so that this small part of Nana can live on!**

MAKES THREE 9-INCH LOAVES

1. To make the starter, in a large bowl, dissolve the yeast in 2½ cups water. Add the potato flakes, sugar, and salt and stir to combine. Cover loosely with plastic wrap and leave the starter out at room temperature for 24 hours.

(continued)

2. Transfer 1 cup of the starter to a separate large bowl, cover loosely, and leave it out at room temperature for 12 hours more. Refrigerate the rest of the starter, covered, and feed it every 3 to 5 days (see Note).

3. To make the bread, lightly grease another large bowl. Add 1½ cups water to the room-temperature starter and stir to combine. Add the flour, oil, sugar, and salt. Knead once or twice in the bowl, then turn out onto a lightly floured surface and knead until a stiff dough forms (add more flour by the quarter-cupful, if needed). Place the dough in the greased bowl, brush the top with oil, and cover loosely with plastic wrap. Leave the dough out at room temperature for 6 to 8 hours, until it has tripled in size.

4. Lightly grease three 9 by 5-inch loaf pans. Turn the dough out onto a lightly floured surface and divide into three equal pieces. Knead each piece once or twice, form into a loaf, and place in the prepared pan. Brush the tops of the loaves with oil and loosely cover with plastic wrap. Leave out at room temperature for 6 to 8 hours, until the dough has again tripled in size. The dough will be puffed over the tops of the pans.

5. Preheat the oven to 350°F. Bake the loaves for 25 to 30 minutes, until the tops are an even golden brown, with no light spots. Allow the loaves to cool in the pans for 20 to 30 minutes, then gently turn them out. Once the bread has cooled completely, cut into thick slices to serve.

NOTE: To feed the starter, combine 1 cup water with ¾ cup sugar and 3 tablespoons potato flakes and stir into the starter. The starter will keep for years if you feed it regularly and keep it refrigerated.

Jodi's Pumpkin-Nut Bread

Jodi is married to Michael's baby brother, Nick, and she's a wonderful baker. This is a perfect fall bread to eat for a snack or to put out with cream cheese on a brunch buffet. Or to give loaves as gifts, like Jodi does.

1¾ cups all-purpose flour

1½ cups sugar

1 teaspoon baking soda

¾ teaspoon salt

½ teaspoon freshly grated nutmeg

½ teaspoon ground cinnamon

1 cup pumpkin puree

2 eggs, lightly beaten

¼ cup vegetable oil

4 tablespoons (½ stick) butter, melted

¾ cup chopped pecans, lightly toasted

Jodi and her daughter, Lauren.

MAKES ONE 9-INCH LOAF

1. Preheat the oven to 350°F. Lightly grease and flour a 9 by 5-inch loaf pan. Sift the flour, sugar, baking soda, salt, nutmeg, and cinnamon into a medium bowl. Make a well in the center and add the pumpkin, eggs, oil, and melted butter. Stir until just combined. Fold in the pecans.

2. Pour the batter into the prepared pan and bake until the bread is golden on top and a sharp knife inserted in the center comes out clean, about 1 hour and 15 minutes. Transfer the pan to a rack and turn the loaf out of the pan once it is cool.

Michelle's Banana-Chocolate Gorilla Bread

3 tablespoons granulated sugar

1 teaspoon ground cinnamon

1 cup packed light brown sugar

8 tablespoons (1 stick) butter

Two 12-ounce tubes refrigerated crescent roll dough

3 tablespoons sweetened condensed milk

2 bananas, sliced ¼-inch thick (48 slices)

4 ounces (about ⅔ cup) semisweet chocolate chips

1½ cups chopped walnuts

Folks, you simply must try Michelle's gorilla bread. It's bigger and better than monkey bread, plus it is so fun to make.

MICHELLE SAYS: **This is something I like if I'm having people over for brunch. I prepare it the night before and bake it just before the party starts, so I can serve it hot.**

SERVES 8

1. Preheat the oven to 350°F. Spray a Bundt pan with nonstick cooking spray. Mix the granulated sugar and cinnamon. In a small saucepan, melt the brown sugar with the butter over low heat.

2. Break open the crescent roll packages and separate the triangles of dough. Brush each triangle with sweetened condensed milk and top with 2 banana slices and 1 teaspoon chocolate chips; fold the edges of the triangle together and seal. Sprinkle each with ¼ teaspoon of the cinnamon sugar.

3. Place half of the walnuts in the pan and top with half of the dough packets. Pour half of the brown sugar–butter mixture over the dough and sprinkle with 2 teaspoons of the cinnamon sugar. Repeat with the remaining ingredients. Bake for 1 hour, until puffed, golden brown, and firm to the touch. Transfer the pan to a rack and allow to cool for 5 minutes. Place a platter on top of the pan and invert. Serve warm.

PB&J Muffins

These are a divine breakfast and a wholesome lunch-box treat. Every time I make them, they take me right back to the PB&J years, when I would cut the crusts off the sandwiches and pack my boys' lunches with a little special treat to remind them how special they are to me.

PAULA'S TIP: **Don't be tempted to use jelly here; it will run too much and leave you with soggy muffins. Use your favorite flavor of good, thick jam instead.**

MAKES 12 MUFFINS

2 cups all-purpose flour

¼ cup packed light brown sugar

2 tablespoons baking powder

½ teaspoon salt

½ cup plus 1 teaspoon creamy peanut butter

1 cup milk

1 egg, lightly beaten

3 tablespoons butter, melted

¼ cup thick jam, such as seedless raspberry

⅓ cup honey-roasted peanuts, chopped

1. Preheat the oven to 350°F. Spray a 12-cup muffin tin with cooking spray. In a food processor, combine the flour, sugar, baking powder, and salt. Pulse in all of the peanut butter until the mixture resembles coarse crumbs. Add the milk, egg, and butter and pulse until combined.

2. Distribute half of the batter equally among the muffin cups. Drop a teaspoonful of jam into each cup and cover with the remaining batter. Top with the chopped peanuts. Bake until the muffins are light golden, 15 to 20 minutes. Transfer them to a wire rack to cool. Serve warm or allow to cool completely and store in an airtight container. The muffins will keep for 1 to 2 days.

Rise and Shine Coffee Crunch Coffee Cake

STREUSEL TOPPING

²/₃ cup baking mix, such as Bisquick

²/₃ cup packed dark brown sugar

¹/₃ cup chopped pecans

1 teaspoon ground cinnamon

¼ teaspoon freshly grated nutmeg

5 tablespoons butter, chilled and diced

CAKE

2 cups baking mix such as Bisquick

2 tablespoons granulated sugar

¹/₃ cup half-and-half

¹/₃ cup brewed coffee

1 egg

2 tablespoons (¼ stick) butter, melted

GLAZE

¾ cup plus 2 tablespoons confectioners' sugar

2 tablespoons brewed coffee

Starting with baking mix is a secret most of the good cooks I know have up their sleeve for making something fresh-baked in the morning. This is one of our favorite eye-openers!

MAKES ONE 9-INCH CAKE, TO SERVE 6 TO 8

1. Preheat the oven to 375°F. Grease a 9-inch springform pan. To make the streusel topping, combine the baking mix, brown sugar, pecans, cinnamon, and nutmeg in a medium bowl. With a pastry cutter or fork, cut in the butter until the mixture resembles large crumbs. Refrigerate until needed.

2. To make the cake, combine the baking mix and granulated sugar in a large bowl or in a food processor. In a separate bowl, whisk together the half-and-half, coffee, egg, and melted butter. Mix or pulse the wet ingredients into the dry until just combined with no dry spots (batter will still be a little lumpy).

3. Fold ¼ cup of the streusel topping into the cake batter. Spread the batter in the pan and cover it with the remaining streusel topping. Bake until the cake is golden and a knife inserted in the center comes out clean, 20 to 25 minutes. Transfer the pan to a wire rack and allow to cool slightly before removing the pan sides and sliding the cake onto a plate.

4. While the cake is cooling, make the glaze. Whisk together the confectioners' sugar and coffee until smooth. Drizzle the glaze over the warm cake and let it set before serving, 15 to 20 minutes.

Easy Blueberry Skillet Coffee Cake

I love to serve a big skillet coffee cake for brunch. It's simple to make, since you start with a tube of biscuit dough, and it's so homey and scrumptious with brown sugar, butter, and blueberries in the pan and an almond streusel on top. If you can time it right, serve it warm from the oven.

SERVES 4 TO 6

1. Preheat the oven to 375°F. To make the streusel, combine the almonds, sugar, butter, flour, and cinnamon in a food processor and pulse until large crumbs form.

2. In a 9-inch cast-iron or other ovenproof skillet, cook the butter and brown sugar over medium heat until melted. Arrange the biscuits in a single layer in the pan; scatter the blueberries over the biscuits and the streusel topping over the berries. Bake until the biscuits are golden and a tester inserted in the center of a biscuit comes out clean, about 30 minutes. Allow to cool slightly and serve from the skillet.

STREUSEL TOPPING

¼ cup slivered almonds

¼ cup granulated sugar

2 tablespoons (¼ stick) butter

2½ tablespoons all-purpose flour

1 teaspoon ground cinnamon

COFFEE CAKE

2 tablespoons (¼ stick) unsalted butter

2 tablespoons light brown sugar

One 12-ounce tube buttermilk biscuits

1 cup blueberries, fresh or thawed frozen

Desserts and Sweets

You may know that I've devoted one of my cookbooks entirely to desserts, and I've *still* got plenty more sweet recipes to share. For one thing, I come from a family of great sweet-toothed bakers. There's my beautiful niece, Corrie, who will exercise her buns off just so she can afford to put away as much dessert as she pleases, and my dear cousin Johnnie, who runs a successful bakery of her own, Gabriel's Desserts, in Marietta, Georgia. And, bless him, I married a man who could make three meals a day off desserts.

Running my restaurant, I learned real quick that just about everyone has a weak spot for some kind of treat at the end of a meal—at least a bite or two of peach cobbler or a couple of cookies, if not the more decadent cakes and pies that we also have on the menu. If food is love, dessert is the sweetest hug and kiss that you can give someone. That's why I make a point of baking a cake for every occasion I can manage.

There's nothing like popping in on a friend and them saying "Would you like a piece of cake?" The answer will always be "Yes, indeed I would." Having a freshly made cake on hand when you've got guests is never a bad idea. You can use a mix and dress it up, or even make a cake from scratch—it's so simple it's hardly any more work than picking up cookies and ice cream at the store. No matter what, making dessert at home means so much more. For one thing, it means you get to lick the batter bowl!

Opposite: Corrie's Carrot-Pecan Cupcakes with Cream Cheese Frosting (page 196).

Corrie's Carrot-Pecan Cupcakes with Cream Cheese Frosting

When her mother and daddy brought my niece, Corrie, home from the hospital, she was only four pounds, but her mother was an RN, so the hospital let her come home because they knew her mother could take care of her as well as they could. Bubba and Jill (his wife at the time and Corrie's mother) put her in my arms and I just started bawling. I fell so in love with that beautiful child. As she grew, her parents let me come and pick her up every Friday night. I'd take her out to dinner. By three years old she was so headstrong, and she just loved to eat. I'd say, "Now, tell me what you want to eat tonight," and she'd say, "I want catpish." And you just hoped you could get a seat at the catfish house.

You know, Corrie shares my love of food. And my relationship with her is much like mine with Aunt Peggy. The three of us are extremely close; we love eating and laughing and spending time together. And naturally, Corrie's a terrific cook. She makes these cupcakes with little dried apricot and mint "carrots" on top that are just like her, so pretty and clever.

CORRIE SAYS: **I love cupcakes. Ever since I was little, they've been my favorite thing. I would look at this cake and think: "It may be small, but it's all mine!"**

PAULA'S TIP: **Use small sprigs of mint that are to scale with the "carrots" for topping these.**

CUPCAKES

3 cups all-purpose flour

3 cups granulated sugar

1 tablespoon baking soda

2 teaspoons ground cinnamon

1 teaspoon salt

1½ cups vegetable oil

4 eggs

1 tablespoon vanilla extract

1½ cups chopped pecans

1½ cups sweetened shredded coconut

1½ cups (three 4-ounce jars) baby food carrots

FROSTING

One 8-ounce package cream cheese, softened

4 tablespoons (½ stick) butter, softened

1 cup confectioners' sugar

½ teaspoon ground cinnamon

GARNISH (OPTIONAL)

¾ cup finely chopped pecans

12 dried apricots

1 bunch fresh mint

1. Preheat the oven to 350°F. Line 18 cups of two regular muffin tins with paper cupcake liners. Sift the flour, granulated sugar, baking soda, cinnamon, and salt into a large bowl. In a separate bowl, whisk together the oil, eggs, and vanilla. Stir the wet ingredients into the dry ingredients. Fold in the pecans, coconut, and carrot puree.

2. Fill the prepared cups halfway. Bake until golden and a tester inserted in the middle of a cupcake comes out clean, about 30 minutes. Let stand for 5 minutes before popping the cupcakes out of the trays to cool completely on wire racks.

3. To make the frosting, beat together the cream cheese, butter, confectioners' sugar, and cinnamon. When the cupcakes are completely cooled, slather the tops with a generous amount of frosting.

4. If you want to garnish the cupcakes, roll the edges of each cupcake in the finely chopped pecans. Slice each dried apricot into 3 small carrot-shaped wedges. Arrange 2 apricot slices on each cupcake, along with mint sprigs to look like carrot tops. Store the cupcakes in an airtight container and keep refrigerated. They will keep for 3 to 4 days.

Fluffy Vanilla Cupcakes with White Chocolate Frosting

Topped with a few berries, these moist cuties with their lavender-colored frosting make great "Happy Birthday" cupcakes.

MAKES 24 CUPCAKES

1. Preheat the oven to 350°F. Grease the cups of two regular muffin tins or line them with paper cupcake liners. In a medium bowl, combine the flour, 1½ cups of the granulated sugar, the baking powder, salt, and baking soda. In a separate bowl, whip the melted butter, egg yolks, buttermilk, vegetable oil, and vanilla until the mixture doubles in volume. Fold the dry ingredients into the egg yolk mixture until the batter is smooth.

2. Using an electric mixer with clean beaters, whip the egg whites and the remaining ¼ cup sugar until stiff peaks form. Fold a large dollop of the meringue into the batter to lighten it, then fold in the rest of the meringue.

3. Fill the prepared cups with batter almost to the top. Bake until the cupcakes are pale gold and a tester inserted in the center of a cupcake comes out clean, about 20 minutes. Transfer the cupcakes to a wire rack to cool.

4. To make the frosting, melt the chocolate and allow it to cool. In a food processor, pulse the blueberries, granulated sugar, and lemon juice until smooth. Cream the confectioners' sugar and butter together until fluffy, add the cooled chocolate, and continue creaming to combine. Add the cream and beat for 1 minute more. Add the blueberry

CUPCAKES

2½ cups cake flour

1¾ cups granulated sugar

1¼ teaspoons baking powder

¾ teaspoon salt

¼ teaspoon baking soda

10 tablespoons (1¼ sticks) butter, melted and cooled

5 egg yolks

1 cup buttermilk

3 tablespoons vegetable oil

1 teaspoon vanilla extract

3 egg whites

FROSTING

6 ounces white chocolate

½ cup blueberries, plus more for garnish

½ teaspoon granulated sugar

1 teaspoon freshly squeezed lemon juice

2 cups confectioners' sugar

½ pound (2 sticks) butter, softened

3 tablespoons heavy cream

mixture and beat just to combine. Spread a generous amount of frosting on each cupcake and serve topped with additional fresh blueberries. Store the cupcakes in an airtight container and keep refrigerated. The cupcakes will keep for 3 to 4 days.

FROSTING

6 tablespoons (¾ stick) butter

⅔ cup packed dark brown sugar

¼ cup heavy cream, plus more if
necessary

2½ cups confectioners' sugar

¾ teaspoon vanilla extract

1 cup chopped pecans, for
garnish

dissolved, 3 to 5 minutes. Remove from the heat and stir in the vanilla. Prick the cooled cakes all over with a toothpick. Spread half the filling on one cake layer. Top with the second layer and repeat.

5. To make the frosting, melt the butter in a small saucepan over medium heat and stir in the brown sugar and cream. Bring the mixture to a simmer and transfer it to a mixing bowl. Add the confectioners' sugar and vanilla and beat until the frosting is a spreadable consistency. Add more cream, 1 tablespoon at a time, if the frosting is too thick. Frost the top of the cake and sprinkle with the chopped pecans. Store in an airtight container at room temperature. The cake will keep for 3 to 5 days.

Charlene Tilton's Brown Derby Grapefruit Cake

Charlene Tilton, that darling sweet girl from the TV show *Dallas*, came on my show to make this cake, which is her version of a layer cake that used to be served at the Brown Derby in Hollywood. And, I'm telling you, it is out of this world. I used to think of grapefruit as diet food—well, not anymore!

MAKES ONE 9-INCH LAYER CAKE, TO SERVE 8 TO 10

1. Preheat the oven to 350°F. Lightly grease a 9-inch round cake pan.

2. To make the cake, sift together the flour, ½ cup of the sugar, the baking powder, and salt into a mixing bowl. Make a well in the dry ingredients and add ¼ cup water, the oil, egg yolks, grapefruit juice, and lemon zest. Using an electric mixer, beat until the mixture is smooth.

3. In a separate bowl, with clean beaters, whip the egg whites until frothy. Add the remaining ¼ cup sugar and the cream of tartar and continue whipping until stiff peaks form. Stir a quarter of the meringue into the egg yolk mixture; then gently fold in the rest of the meringue to combine.

4. Pour the batter into the prepared pan and bake for 25 to 30 minutes, until the sides of the cake begin to pull away from the pan and the middle bounces back when gently pressed. Allow the cake to cool in the pan for 10 minutes, then gently turn it out onto a wire rack.

5. While the cake is cooling, make the frosting. Beat the cream cheese, grapefruit juice, and lemon zest until light and

CAKE

1½ cups cake flour, sifted

¾ cup granulated sugar

1½ teaspoons baking powder

½ teaspoon salt

¼ cup vegetable oil

3 eggs, separated

3 tablespoons freshly squeezed grapefruit juice, strained

½ teaspoon finely grated lemon zest

¼ teaspoon cream of tartar

FROSTING

12 ounces cream cheese (1½ eight-ounce packages)

2 tablespoons freshly squeezed grapefruit juice, strained

1 tablespoon finely grated lemon zest

¾ cup confectioners' sugar

1 pound canned red or fresh white or red grapefruit sections (about 3½ grapefruits), pith removed and syrup drained if using canned

4 to 6 drops red food coloring (optional)

fluffy. Gradually beat in the confectioners' sugar. Beat in two sections of the grapefruit and the food coloring (if using) one drop at a time until the desired pink color is reached.

6. To assemble, cut the cake in half horizontally to make two layers. Cover the bottom layer with about one third of the frosting. Arrange half the grapefruit sections around the edge of the cake layer. Top with the remaining cake layer and cover the top and sides with the remaining frosting. Arrange the remaining grapefruit sections in a circle in the middle of the cake. Store wrapped or in an airtight container in the refrigerator. The cake will keep for 3 to 5 days.

Fluffy Southern Coconut and Lemon Curd Cake

I've been making coconut cake for Jamie's birthday since who knows when. I find a good, tart lemon buttercream is the nicest match for this fluffy, delicious cake.

MAKES ONE 8-INCH 4-LAYER CAKE, TO SERVE 8

1. Preheat the oven to 350°F. Grease and flour two 8-inch round cake pans. Prepare and bake the cake according to the package directions. Let the cakes cool in the pans for 10 minutes, then turn them out onto a wire rack to cool completely.

2. To make the frosting, in a heatproof bowl or in the top of a double boiler, combine the sugar, egg whites, cream of tartar, salt, and ⅓ cup water. Place the bowl over boiling water (don't let the bottom of the bowl touch the water or the frosting could get grainy) and beat with an electric mixer for 1 minute. Take the bowl away from the heat and continue to beat with an electric mixer for an additional 7 minutes on high speed.

3. Heat the lemon curd gently over medium-low heat (or microwave for 20 seconds on medium power), just to soften. Fold the curd and lemon zest into the frosting.

4. To assemble the cake, cut each layer in half horizontally. Frost one layer and top it with the next, using all the layers. Frost the top and sides of the cake and cover with the coconut. Store wrapped or in an airtight container in the refrigerator. The cake will keep for 3 to 5 days.

CAKE

One 18¼-ounce box lemon cake mix

FROSTING

1½ cups sugar

2 egg whites

¼ teaspoon cream of tartar

⅛ teaspoon salt

One 11-ounce jar lemon curd

Finely grated zest of 1 lemon

1½ cups sweetened flaked coconut

Peaches and Cream Shortcakes

3 pounds (about 12) peaches, pitted and sliced

3 tablespoons packed light brown sugar

2¾ cups all-purpose flour

4 teaspoons baking powder

½ teaspoon salt

12 tablespoons (1½ sticks) butter, chilled and cubed, plus 1 tablespoon butter, melted

2 eggs, lightly beaten

One 8-ounce container sour cream

2 teaspoons vanilla extract

Whipped cream, for garnish

When the peaches are ripe in Georgia, I always march right past the baskets of perfect round fruits and head for the bruised ones on special. Y'all, I promise that's where that smell of ripe, syrup-sweet peach is coming from, and if you're cooking them that same day, those are the ones you want. This is a quick, delicious dessert to make on a hot Southern summer night.

MAKES 12 SHORTCAKES

1. Preheat the oven to 450°F. Lightly grease a baking sheet. In a large bowl, combine the peaches with the brown sugar and let sit for at least 20 minutes.

2. In a separate bowl, combine the flour, baking powder, and salt. Using a pastry cutter or fork, cut in the cubed butter until large crumbs form.

3. Whisk together the eggs, sour cream, and vanilla; fold into the dry ingredients until just combined. Drop the dough by the quarter-cup onto the baking sheet. Brush the tops with the melted butter. Bake until golden, about 12 minutes. Allow to cool.

4. Split the shortcakes in half horizontally. Spoon about ½ cup of the peach mixture onto the bottom half of each shortcake and cover with the top half, like a lid. Serve with a generous dollop of whipped cream. Assemble the shortcakes to order. If you have leftovers, store the peaches, shortcakes, and whipped cream in separate containers in the refrigerator. They'll keep for 2 to 3 days.

Bourbon-Bathed Brown Sugar Pound Cake

I've made so many pound cakes in my life, I could make one in my sleep. (Come to think of it, I could probably eat one in my sleep, too!) This version, made with brown sugar, is what I take over to welcome a new neighbor. Soaked with a yummy bourbon syrup, it's a great get-to-know-you cake.

MAKES ONE 10-INCH CAKE, TO SERVE 10 TO 12

POUND CAKE

¾ pound (3 sticks) butter

One 16-ounce package dark brown sugar (2¼ packed cups)

1 cup granulated sugar

5 eggs

3½ cups cake flour

½ teaspoon baking powder

1 cup milk

2 tablespoons bourbon

1½ teaspoons vanilla extract

¼ teaspoon freshly grated nutmeg

BOURBON SYRUP

6 tablespoons granulated sugar

3 tablespoons bourbon

1. Preheat the oven to 325°F. Grease and flour a 10-inch Bundt pan. Using an electric mixer, cream the butter. Add the sugars, 1 cup at a time, and continue to beat until smooth. Add the eggs, one at a time, beating well after each addition.

2. Sift together the flour and baking powder. Add in three batches to the butter mixture, alternating with the milk. Add the bourbon, vanilla, and nutmeg; mix well.

3. Pour the batter into the prepared pan. Bake until the cake is dark golden and a tester inserted in the center comes out clean, about 1½ hours. Allow the cake to cool in the pan for 20 minutes and then turn it out on a wire rack to finish cooling.

4. To make the bourbon syrup, simmer the sugar with ½ cup water in a small saucepan until the sugar dissolves. Remove the pan from the heat. Once the mixture cools, stir in the bourbon. With a toothpick, poke holes in the top of the cake and slowly pour the syrup over the holes. Use a pastry brush to soak the sides with additional syrup. Let stand until completely cool, about 1 hour, before serving. Store wrapped or in an airtight container at room temperature. The cake will keep for 3 to 5 days.

Coconut Cream Bread Pudding with Chocolate Velvet Sauce

BREAD PUDDING

One 16- to 20-inch loaf French bread, cut into 1-inch cubes

4 egg yolks

2 whole eggs

Two 13.5- to 14.5-ounce cans unsweetened coconut milk

One 15-ounce can cream of coconut

¼ teaspoon salt

¼ teaspoon freshly grated nutmeg

Pinch of mace

2 cups sweetened flaked coconut

CHOCOLATE SAUCE

1 cup (6 ounces) semisweet chocolate chips

½ cup heavy cream

We've been making the same bread pudding at The Lady & Sons for so long I almost got sick of it one day. Almost. So to mix things up, I created this one. The rich coconut pudding with a nice pool of chocolate sauce all around brings me back to the days when me and Bubba would count out all our change to buy Mounds bars on the way home from school.

SERVES 6

1. Lightly grease the bottom of a 9-inch square flameproof baking dish. Arrange the bread cubes evenly in the dish. In a large bowl, whisk together the yolks and whole eggs, coconut milk, cream of coconut, salt, nutmeg, and mace. Stir in 1½ cups of the coconut flakes. Pour the custard over the bread cubes. Press the bread cubes gently to soak up the custard. Let the mixture stand for 1 hour, covered, in the refrigerator.

2. Preheat the oven to 325°F. Sprinkle the top of the pudding with the remaining ½ cup coconut flakes. Cover the baking dish with foil, poking a few holes to release the steam. Place a roasting pan on the oven rack and put the baking dish in it. Pour hot water into the roasting pan to come halfway up the sides of the baking dish. Bake until the pudding is firm to the touch, about 1 hour and 15 minutes. Remove the foil and bake for 15 minutes more. Remove the baking dish from the water bath and run it under the broiler, at least 4 inches from

(continued)

the heat, until golden, 1 to 2 minutes. Let the pudding cool completely. Cover tightly with plastic wrap and refrigerate.

3. Make the chocolate sauce right before serving the pudding. Place the chocolate chips in a medium heatproof bowl. In a small saucepan, bring the cream to a simmer; immediately remove it from the heat and pour it over the chocolate chips. Whisk until smooth. Pour the sauce over individual pudding servings, as desired. The chocolate sauce can be reheated in a saucepan over low heat. Add more cream, 1 tablespoon at a time as needed, to return it to the desired consistency.

Baked Chocolate Custard Cups with Butterscotch Whipped Cream

CUSTARD

1 cup (6 ounces) semisweet
    chocolate chips

1 cup heavy cream

1 cup milk

4 egg yolks

3 tablespoons sugar

Pinch of salt

WHIPPED CREAM

1 cup heavy cream

3 tablespoons butterscotch
    pudding mix (not instant,
    and with sugar)

My Grandmama Paul made pies and cakes whether or not there was a special occasion, so a chocolate pudding was just a casual weeknight sweet to her. I love the old-fashioned taste of a good pudding, and I love to spoon my luscious butterscotch whipped cream over it.

PAULA'S TIP: **The butterscotch whipped cream is also delicious over a warm brownie, a bowl of coffee ice cream, or a piece of peach pie.**

SERVES 6

1. Preheat the oven to 300°F. Place the chocolate chips in a medium heatproof bowl. Bring the cream and milk to a boil in a medium saucepan over medium heat. Pour the hot cream mixture over the chocolate and whisk until smooth.

2. In a large bowl, whisk together the egg yolks, sugar, and salt. Whisking constantly, pour the chocolate mixture into the egg mixture. Strain the custard through a fine-mesh sieve and divide it among six 4-ounce ramekins.

3. Place the ramekins in a large roasting pan. Carefully pour hot water into the pan to come halfway up the sides of the ramekins. Cover the pan tightly with foil; poke a few small holes in the foil for steam to escape. Bake on the center rack

(continued)

for 30 to 35 minutes, until the edges of the custard are slightly set but the center still jiggles (the center will set as the pudding cools). Remove the ramekins from the water bath and allow them to cool completely, then refrigerate them for at least 3 hours before serving.

4. To make the butterscotch whipped cream, whisk the cream and pudding powder together in a bowl, just to combine. Let stand for about 5 minutes, until the powder begins to dissolve. Using an electric mixer, beat on medium-high speed until thickened. Top each custard cup with a generous dollop of whipped cream before serving. Wrap untopped custard cups in plastic and refrigerate.

Souffléed Grits Pudding

I tend to eat grits with sausage or shrimp, but, you know, there's no reason to think of them as only a savory food. So lately I've been playing around with dessert recipes that have grits in them, and this one was a winner. I think Jamie polished off about half of it when I asked him what he thought. This pudding is perfect for brunch, too, and you can have your sausage right alongside it!

SERVES 4

3 tablespoons butter, plus more for the soufflé dish

½ cup plus 2 tablespoons sugar, plus more for the soufflé dish

2½ cups milk

1 cup half-and-half

1 cup regular grits (not quick-cooking or instant)

Pinch of salt

1 tablespoon brandy

1 teaspoon finely grated lemon zest

½ teaspoon ground cinnamon

½ teaspoon freshly grated nutmeg

3 eggs, separated

1. Preheat the oven to 400°F. Butter the bottom and sides of a 2-quart soufflé dish and coat the surface evenly with sugar, tapping out the excess.

2. In a medium saucepan, combine the milk, half-and-half, the ½ cup sugar, and the 3 tablespoons butter. Bring the mixture to a boil over medium-high heat. Very slowly, to avoid lumps, whisk in the grits and salt. Reduce the heat and simmer, stirring constantly, until the mixture is thickened and cooked through, about 15 minutes. Transfer the grits to a large bowl and stir in the brandy, lemon zest, cinnamon, and nutmeg. Allow to cool for at least 15 minutes.

3. Stir the egg yolks into the grits. Using an electric mixer, whip the egg whites to soft peaks, add the 2 tablespoons sugar, and continue whipping until stiff peaks form. Fold in one third of the meringue to lighten the grits, then fold in the remaining meringue. Scrape the batter into the prepared soufflé dish and bake on the center oven rack until the soufflé is golden but the center still jiggles, 40 to 45 minutes. Serve immediately.

Blackberry–Almond Crunch Crumble

FILLING

8 cups fresh blackberries

⅓ cup granulated sugar

1 tablespoon quick-cooking tapioca (optional)

½ teaspoon finely grated lemon zest

CRUMBLE TOPPING

1¾ cups all-purpose flour

⅓ cup packed dark brown sugar

⅓ cup granulated sugar

1 teaspoon ground cinnamon

1 teaspoon ground ginger

⅛ teaspoon salt

8 tablespoons (1 stick) butter, melted

½ cup finely chopped almonds (with skins, not blanched)

My mama and daddy used to make us fresh ice cream in the summer, and we gobbled it up without thinking what lucky kids we were. But, you know, I can still remember the exact taste of that ice cream, with fresh blackberries tossed in sugar and churned in right at the end. I like to top this crumble with a scoop of vanilla for a little piece of that heaven.

SERVES 6

1. Preheat the oven to 350°F. To make the filling, in a bowl, toss the berries with the sugar, tapioca (if using), and lemon zest. Pour the mixture into an ungreased 9-inch square or round baking dish.

2. To make the topping, in a large bowl, whisk together the flour, sugars, cinnamon, ginger, and salt. Stir in the butter and almonds.

3. Using your fingers, rub the topping mixture into coarse crumbs and sprinkle it over the filling. Bake for about 1 hour, until the filling bubbles and the topping is light golden brown. Allow the crumble to cool slightly before serving.

Autumn Harvest Crunch-Top Pie

CRUMB TOPPING

1 cup all-purpose flour

½ cup packed light brown sugar

1 teaspoon ground cinnamon

½ teaspoon freshly grated nutmeg

½ teaspoon ground ginger

¼ teaspoon salt

8 tablespoons (1 stick) butter, chilled and cut into ½-inch dice

½ cup finely chopped walnuts

PIE

½ cup dried cranberries

½ cup dark raisins

¼ cup dark rum or apple cider

1 cup sour cream

2 eggs

⅔ cup packed light brown sugar

3 pounds mixed apples, such as Granny Smith, Golden Delicious, and McIntosh, peeled, cored, and thinly sliced

1 unbaked 9-inch piecrust

I like to call this my back-to-school pie. When I smell those apples baking with all those yummy spices, I feel like grabbing my book bag and my pom-poms and heading out to catch the bus!

MAKES ONE 9-INCH PIE, TO SERVE 6

1. To prepare the topping, in a medium bowl, whisk together the flour, brown sugar, cinnamon, nutmeg, ginger, and salt. Using a pastry cutter or fork, cut in the butter to form large crumbs. Stir in the walnuts. Chill, covered, until needed.

2. Preheat the oven to 350°F. Line a rimmed baking sheet with foil. In a small saucepan, combine the cranberries, raisins, dark rum, and 2 tablespoons water; bring to a boil over medium-high heat, then remove the pan from the heat and allow to cool completely.

3. In a medium bowl, whisk together the sour cream, eggs, and brown sugar. Stir in the dried fruit mixture and apples. Arrange the crust in a pie plate. Fill the crust with the apple mixture, mounding the filling so it is slightly higher in the center. Place the pie on the prepared baking sheet and bake for 45 minutes.

4. Remove the pie from the oven and increase the temperature to 425°F. Scatter the topping over the pie. Bake for 20 to 30 minutes more, until the topping is golden and the juices are bubbling. Serve warm.

Two-Berry Chess Pie

This is my twist on the classic chess pie, an old-fashioned cornmeal dessert that my great-grandmama probably made—you can find it in some of the oldest Southern cookbooks. Juicy berries and a little bit of Grand Marnier make it taste fresh and not the least bit outdated!

MAKES ONE 9-INCH PIE, TO SERVE 6 TO 8

1. Preheat the oven to 350°F. Using an electric mixer, cream the sugars and butter. Beat in the eggs, one at a time. Scrape down the sides of the bowl; beat in the milk, flour, vanilla, and salt until smooth.

2. Pour the mixture into the crust and bake until the filling is dark golden and just set (the center will still jiggle), 40 to 45 minutes. Let the pie stand at room temperature until completely cooled.

3. In a small saucepan, heat the apricot jam over medium-low heat until melted, about 3 minutes. Strain the jam into a small bowl and stir in the Grand Marnier. Sprinkle the berries evenly over the top of the pie. Brush the berries with the apricot glaze and serve.

1 cup granulated sugar

1 cup packed light brown sugar

4 tablespoons (½ stick) butter, softened

4 eggs

⅓ cup milk

2 tablespoons all-purpose flour

1½ teaspoons vanilla extract

Pinch of salt

One 9-inch graham cracker crust

¼ cup apricot jam

1 tablespoon Grand Marnier

1 pint raspberries

1 pint blackberries

Charlye's Favorite "Punkin" Chiffon Pie

One 9-inch frozen deep-dish
   piecrust

32 jumbo marshmallows

1 cup pumpkin puree

½ teaspoon pumpkin pie spice

¼ teaspoon salt

One 12-ounce container Cool
   Whip

Cousin Charlye is my Aunt Trina's younger daughter, and this is her very favorite pie. I can't remember how it made its way into our family holiday, but Charlye just insists on it every Thanksgiving, and has since she was little enough to call pumpkins "punkins." No one's complaining, though. This pie is sweet, fluffy, and delicious, and it couldn't be easier to make.

PAULA'S TIP: **I like to do as much of my Thanksgiving cooking as possible a few days ahead, but this pie is really best on the day it is made. Good thing it's so quick to make!**

MAKES ONE 9-INCH PIE, TO SERVE 6

1. Bake the piecrust according to the package directions and allow to cool.

2. In the top of a double boiler over low heat, combine the marshmallows and the pumpkin puree. Using a heatproof spatula, stir the mixture constantly until the marshmallows are melted. Take the pan off the heat and stir in the spice and salt.

3. When the mixture is completely cool, stir in half the Cool Whip. Pour the filling into the prepared piecrust and spread with the remainder of the whipped topping to serve.

CRUST

3 cups graham cracker crumbs (about 22 crackers)

9 tablespoons (1 stick plus 1 tablespoon) butter, melted

½ cup sugar

FILLING

2 pounds (four 8-ounce packages) cream cheese, softened

1½ cups sugar

2 tablespoons cornstarch

One 16-ounce container sour cream

½ cup freshly squeezed orange juice

½ teaspoon vanilla extract

5 eggs

TOPPING

8 tablespoons (1 stick) butter

1½ pounds (about 3 large) Golden Delicious apples, peeled, cored, and cut into ½-inch cubes

½ cup chopped pecans

1 cup sugar

½ cup heavy cream

Cousin Johnnie's Caramel-Apple Cheesecake

Leave it to my cousin Johnnie, the baker. Her cheesecakes are all over-the-top delicious, and the caramel-apple is my all-time favorite.

COUSIN JOHNNIE SAYS: **The easiest way to do a water bath for this recipe is to add the water to the pan after placing it in the oven. That way it won't splash the cake when you move it from the counter. It's not a must to bake this in a water bath; if you skip this step, it will take 15 to 20 minutes less time, but I do love the extra creaminess that a water bath–baked cheesecake has.**

MAKES ONE 10-INCH CHEESECAKE, TO SERVE 16

1. Preheat the oven to 350°F. Wrap the bottom and sides of a 10-inch springform pan tightly with foil to prevent moisture from the water bath from seeping into the cheesecake.

2. To make the crust, in a food processor, mix the graham cracker crumbs, butter, and sugar. Press the mixture into the bottom and halfway up the sides of the prepared pan. Bake the crust for 10 minutes, then remove it from the oven to cool completely.

3. While the crust cools, make the filling. In a food processor or with an electric mixer, mix the cream cheese, sugar, and cornstarch until smooth. Add the sour cream, orange juice, and vanilla and blend until smooth. Beat in the eggs one at a time, blending until just combined.

4. Pour the filling into the crust. Place a roasting pan on a rack in the center of the oven and transfer the cheesecake pan to it. Fill the roasting pan with hot water to come halfway up the sides of the cake pan and cover it loosely with foil. Bake until the center moves only slightly when the cake pan is shaken, about 1 hour and 45 minutes. Check the water level about an hour into baking, adding more if needed. Carefully remove the cake from the oven and roasting pan to cool. Refrigerate overnight.

5. To make the topping, melt the butter in a large skillet over high heat. Add the apples and pecans and cook, stirring, until they are coated with butter, about 2 minutes. Add the sugar and stir until the sugar dissolves and the liquid comes to a boil, about 3 minutes.

6. Using a slotted spoon, transfer the apples and pecans to a bowl. Reduce the heat to medium-high and cook the remaining liquid, stirring often, until it turns a deep amber, about 6 minutes. Remove the skillet from the heat to stop the cooking and add the cream. Be careful, as the cream may splatter. Return the skillet to the heat and bring it to a boil, whisking constantly. Remove the sauce from the heat and stir in the apples and pecans. Allow to cool until lukewarm.

7. Spread the caramel-apple mixture evenly over the top of the cheesecake. Refrigerate until ready to serve. Use a knife dipped in hot water to cut through the caramel mixture.

Bubba's Tiny Chocolate–Key Lime Pies

The number one best-selling dessert at Uncle Bubba's Oyster House is Key lime pie, and these are just a tiny version of that pie with a chocolate twist. They're perfect at parties as finger food, when you need just a little something sweet after dinner. And you can make them two days ahead and just leave them in the fridge until serving—which is great when the rest of the meal needs your more immediate attention.

MAKES 30 TINY PIES

½ pound (2 sticks) butter, melted, plus more for greasing pans

1¾ cups (9 ounces) chocolate wafer cookie crumbs

¾ cup sugar

One 14-ounce can sweetened condensed milk

¼ cup freshly squeezed Key lime juice or regular lime juice

3 egg yolks, lightly beaten

Finely grated zest of 2 Key limes or 1 regular lime

1 teaspoon vanilla extract

Pinch of salt

Whipped cream, for serving

Milk chocolate curls, for serving (Use an 8-ounce bar of chocolate at room temperature. Shave curls with a vegetable peeler and use immediately or refrigerate.)

1. Preheat the oven to 325°F. Lightly brush 30 cups of two mini-muffin pans with melted butter. Fill the unused cups halfway up with water. In a medium bowl, combine the cookie crumbs, butter, and sugar. Press about 1 tablespoon of the cookie mixture into each mini-muffin cup, making sure there are no cracks. Bake the piecrusts for 10 minutes.

2. In a large bowl, whisk together the condensed milk, Key lime juice, egg yolks, lime zest, vanilla extract, and salt. Spoon 1 even tablespoon of filling into each warm piecrust. Bake the pies until the filling is set, 20 to 25 minutes.

3. Transfer the muffin pans to a cooling rack and let stand for 20 minutes at room temperature. Use a small offset spatula or butter knife to carefully unmold the pies from the pans. When the pies are completely cool, top each with a dollop of whipped cream and decorate with a milk chocolate curl. Store untopped pies, wrapped or in an airtight container, in the refrigerator.

Easy Watermelon Sherbet

¾ cup sugar

Juice of 1 lime

Pinch of salt

3½ pounds (about 6 cups) seedless watermelon cubes

When I started my businesses selling sandwiches office-to-office, I just did not know how much cooking I'd be doing, for how many long, long hours. I'm glad I never had a chance to stop and think once the work picked up, because I might have thought I couldn't keep up the pace. Well, I have, but you know me, I'm never one to avoid using whatever conveniences I can to make great food without working my tail off! And when I hit on a simple recipe like this sherbet, I stick with it. It's the perfect thing on a hot night, and it's easy enough to make even when the summer weather has you feeling like you can hardly put one foot in front of the other.

MAKES 1 QUART

1. In a small pot, simmer the sugar with ¾ cup water, stirring occasionally, until the sugar dissolves. Allow it to cool. In a small bowl, stir together the lime juice and salt.

2. In a food processor, in batches if necessary, puree the watermelon until smooth. Pour the puree into a large bowl. Stir in the sugar syrup and the lime juice mixture. Pour the mixture into an ice cream maker and churn according to the manufacturer's directions. Store in an airtight container in the freezer.

VARIATION: Don't have an ice cream maker? Try this variation, a watermelon granita: Mix the syrup and watermelon puree according to the directions and transfer the mixture to a shallow metal baking pan. Cover the pan and place it in the freezer. Stir every 45 minutes until frozen, about 3 hours. Cover the granita and keep it frozen until ready to serve.

Strawberry-Banana Ice Pops

I can't recall how I got into making ice pops for the boys, but recently I found the freezer molds I used and they brought back such strong memories of two little messy-haired fellows just jumping up and down and begging me for freezer pops! I made up some of these strawberry-banana pops for me and Michael just to relive those memories, and I can't wait to make them for my grandson, Jack, someday soon.

MAKES 8 POPS

One 3¼-ounce package instant banana cream pudding mix (regular, not sugar-free)

1¾ cups milk

2 cups sliced strawberries

1 tablespoon sugar

In a blender, combine all the ingredients and blend until smooth. Pour into ice pop molds and freeze for at least 4 hours. If you don't have molds, divide among 8 small plastic or paper cups (5-ounce cups are a good size), cover each with plastic wrap, and pop a wooden stick through the wrap.

Beverages

Other than a frosty glass of Minty Southern Sweet Tea (page 245) or maybe some Sparkling Sweet Cherry Lemonade (page 246) on a hot afternoon, I think of drinks as party material. A glass of something festive that you took the trouble to make (and let's be honest, it's hardly ever any trouble to throw a few things into a pitcher) tells your guests that it's time to relax and enjoy themselves.

The rest of my family tends to be in charge of the bar, maybe because I have a tendency to get so wrapped up in my cooking I hardly stop to think drinks. So while I'm deciding to make just one more batch of biscuits in case everyone's especially hungry (and aren't they always?), someone else ends up taking drink orders. And they've created some mighty tasty concoctions over the years, I must say. Just wait till you have an occasion to try my boys' Holiday Butterscotch Egg-nog (page 254); it is truly divine.

Then there's coffee. Now, that's a different matter. When I was growing up, my mama and daddy drank instant Sanka. I suppose since there was never, ever, a pot of coffee around, I just never acquired a taste for it. Not until Michael moved in, that is. Michael loves good coffee. Working as a harbor captain, he has the opportunity to go on board boats coming in from all over the world. As soon as you step onto the deck of a boat, someone always offers you coffee. And Michael, well, he never refuses a good, strong cup of fresh-brewed joe.

That man loves good coffee so much, I wasn't surprised when he came home

Opposite: Iced Mocha Frappé (page 250).

243

one day and announced, "I'm going to start me a line of coffee." "You go ahead, sweetie," I told him, "but you're going to be on your own because I wouldn't know a good cup of coffee if it hit me." He just smiled and said, "That's too bad, because you're going to be a coffee drinker now!" And don't you know, I can't get enough—I even started making up my own recipes for coffee done my way (you know I can never resist), like my Cinnamon-Orange Cappuccino (page 249). Michael has introduced me to so many new things, and his coffee is certainly one of the most eye-opening!

Minty Southern Sweet Tea

7 tea bags (black leaf, such as
   Lipton)

1 small bunch fresh mint, plus
   extra leaves, for garnish

1 cup sugar

My daddy always said, "Nobody makes sweet tea as good as Mama's." I reckon the tea that's sugared by your sweetheart will always rate best, so serve a refreshing glass to the ones you love.

MAKES ABOUT 2 QUARTS

1. In a large pot, bring 4 cups water to a boil. Add the tea bags and mint; stir. Let the tea steep for 1 hour. Remove the tea bags.

2. In a medium saucepan, bring 1 cup water and the sugar to a boil; simmer, stirring occasionally, for 5 minutes or until the sugar dissolves. Let the syrup cool for 15 minutes, then pour it into the tea. Add 4 cups cold water and stir to combine. Transfer the tea to a large pitcher. Serve the tea over ice, garnished with mint leaves.

Sparkling Sweet Cherry Lemonade

If you ever find yourself getting tired of the same old lemonade summer after summer, here's the solution. This recipe's got a beautiful ruby red color from the cherries and tastes like a burst of fruit. We like to make fizzy lemonade sodas by using bubbly water, but you can use flat water for regular lemonade, too. Pull up a porch swing and enjoy!

MAKES ABOUT 2 QUARTS

One 10-ounce package frozen pitted sweet cherries (2 cups), thawed

1 cup freshly squeezed lemon juice

1 cup sugar

5 cups chilled seltzer, plus more to taste

In a blender, puree the cherries, lemon juice, and sugar. Pour the mixture into a large pitcher. Add the seltzer and stir gently. Pour into glasses over ice and top with additional seltzer, if desired.

Brooke, Jack, and Jaime.

Michael's Irish Coffee

Michael is a black-coffee connoisseur, but he's not above spicing up his coffee with whiskey and a pinch of ginger. Honey, Irish coffee is the perfect nightcap for when you're ready to go to bed but not to sleep!

SERVES 4

1 cup heavy cream

4½ ounces (9 tablespoons) Irish whiskey

⅛ teaspoon ground ginger

3 cups hot brewed coffee

8 teaspoons sugar, or to taste

1. Whip the cream to soft peaks; fold in 1 tablespoon of the whiskey and the ginger until combined.

2. Divide the coffee among four cups. Stir 2 tablespoons of the whiskey and 2 teaspoons of the sugar, or sugar to taste, into each cup. Top each with a generous dollop of the whipped cream and serve immediately.

Cinnamon-Orange Cappuccino

2²/₃ cups whole milk

Three 3-inch strips orange peel

Two 2½-inch cinnamon sticks,
  broken in half

Four 2-ounce espresso cups hot
  brewed espresso

Sugar

One variety in Michael's line of coffee is called "Full Steam Ahead" and it's so darn rich and good that it's become my absolute favorite. I used it to make some cappuccino at Christmas last year, and it's already a family tradition for the holidays.

MICHAEL SAYS: **When the big container ships and tankers come into Savannah, I go on board and direct the tugboats how to dock them. Now, every time you get aboard a ship, they ask if you would like something to drink. And because I work a lot of long hours onboard, I always take coffee. We've got Greek ships come in, Turkish ships, Italian ships, so you get cappuccino, or a little cup of Greek or Turkish coffee (which taste about the same to me, but don't tell that to a Greek or a Turk). And my brother got me into drinking Cuban coffee, which is like a super-espresso with a lot of sugar in it—almost prescription coffee. So over the years I've become a coffee connoisseur, and it just made sense that I'd start my own coffee company.**

SERVES 4

1. Place the milk, orange peel, and cinnamon sticks in a small saucepan over medium-low heat and simmer gently for 5 minutes. Cover and let stand off the heat for 2 minutes.

2. Remove the orange peel and cinnamon sticks and, using a frother or wire whisk, whisk the mixture until foamy.

3. Divide the espresso among four serving cups. Spoon the froth onto the espresso. Sprinkle with sugar, as desired.

Iced Mocha Frappé

If you've got tall parfait glasses and iced tea spoons, pull them out for this soda fountain treat.

SERVES 2 TO 4

1. Stir the hot chocolate mix and sugar into the coffee until dissolved. Pour the mixture into ice cube trays. Freeze, covered, for at least 3 hours and up to 1 week.

2. Put the frozen cubes in a blender. Add the cream and vanilla and puree until smooth. Divide among tall glasses and top with whipped cream.

Four 1-ounce packages hot chocolate mix (¾ cup mix)

¼ cup sugar

4 cups hot brewed coffee

1 cup heavy cream, half-and-half, or whole milk

2 teaspoons vanilla extract

Whipped cream, for serving

Hot Spiced Apple-Pear Cider

4 cups apple cider

4 cups pear juice or nectar

4 teaspoons dark brown sugar

Two 2½-inch cinnamon sticks

4 whole cloves

4 black peppercorns

4 allspice berries

I remember reading an article that suggested boiling a pot of water with apples, pears, and a cinnamon stick during the holidays to fill your house with a festive aroma. Well, I thought, that's a nice waste of perfectly good ingredients. This cozy winter drink does indeed make your home smell delicious, and, better yet, you can offer your guests a warm mugful.

SERVES 8

Place all the ingredients in a saucepan and simmer over medium heat for 5 minutes. Let steep, off the heat, for at least 20 minutes. Reheat, then strain and serve.

Cousin Johnnie's White Sangria with Peaches

You know that gorgeous perfume that comes off a ripe peach? Well, here it is in a punch bowl. Take it from me: This sangria tastes like a summer breeze, but it'll knock you flat if you're not looking! My cousin Johnnie Gabriel, who owns Gabriel's Desserts in Marietta, Georgia, sent me the recipe, and it's a keeper.

JOHNNIE SAYS: **This is fabulous! I make it when we have our Gabriel's Desserts employee party at our house each year. We've made it a tradition to have dinner and pack gifts for needy children. The recipe was shared with me by the owner of Fusco's Via Roma, a restaurant in Acworth, Georgia.**

One 750-ml bottle white wine, such as Pinot Grigio

¾ cup Grand Marnier

¾ cup brandy

1 tablespoon sugar

¾ pound (about 2 cups) peaches, preferably white, pitted and cubed

1 liter ginger ale, chilled

SERVES 12 TO 16

1. In a 2-quart pitcher, mix the wine, Grand Marnier, brandy, and sugar, stirring until the sugar is dissolved. Add the peaches and let stand for 1 hour in the refrigerator.

2. Spoon the peaches into the bottoms of twelve wine-glasses. Pour the cold wine mixture over them. Top off each serving with ¼ cup ginger ale, or more to taste. Enjoy!

Brooke's Pretty Pomegranate Spritzers

1 lemon, for twists

2 cups ginger ale, chilled

1 cup pomegranate juice, chilled

Ice cubes

1 cup seltzer, or more to taste

Brooke came up with this nonalcoholic drink when she was expecting baby Jack, and we all became fond of it. It's pretty and pink and perfect at brunch. If you want to try a more traditional version with wine, see the variation below.

SERVES 6

1. To make lemon twists for the garnish, use a vegetable peeler to remove strips of peel from the lemon, leaving as much white pith on the lemon as possible.

2. In a pitcher, combine the ginger ale and pomegranate juice. Fill six wineglasses with ice. Divide the liquid among the glasses, leaving room for seltzer. Pour the seltzer into each glass, to taste. Twist the peel and rub a strip on the edge of each glass. Drop the twist into the drink and serve.

VARIATION: Substitute dry white wine for the seltzer.

Jamie and Bobby's Holiday Butterscotch Eggnog

The boys make this every year, and they leave the liquor on the side for those who want it. It's a dessert in a glass and I always look forward to sipping a cup by the tree.

PAULA'S TIP: **If you don't want to waste egg whites and you don't have a problem with raw eggs, you can beat the egg whites and fold them into the eggnog in place of the cream. It makes it lighter, too. Just remember, raw eggs should not be eaten by the very young, the very old, pregnant women, or anyone with a compromised immune system.**

4 cups milk

8 egg yolks

²⁄₃ cup packed light brown sugar

¹⁄₈ teaspoon salt

4 teaspoons vanilla extract

½ cup heavy cream

¼ cup bourbon (optional)

2 tablespoons brandy (optional)

Freshly grated nutmeg, for garnish

SERVES 12

1. Heat the milk to a slow boil in a medium saucepan over medium-low heat. In a large bowl, whisk the yolks and brown sugar until thick. Whisking constantly, slowly pour the milk into the sugar mixture until fully incorporated. Whisk in the salt. Return the mixture to the pot over medium heat. Cook, stirring constantly with a spatula or wooden spoon, scraping the bottom and sides of the pot, until the mixture is thick enough to coat the back of the spoon, 5 to 10 minutes. Strain through a fine-mesh sieve into a large bowl and allow to cool to lukewarm before stirring in the vanilla.

2. Whip the cream until soft peaks form and fold it into the custard. Add the bourbon and brandy (if using). Garnish with nutmeg and serve.

The Bald Man's Workaholic's Hot Chocolate

My hardworking, chocolate-obsessed friend Oded Brenner, who with Max Fichtman started the Chocolate by the Bald Man restaurants (and created "Max Brenner"), made this deliciously thick and creamy hot chocolate on my show. I make it as a treat whenever we have children around—and adults love it, too.

SERVES 4

1. In a small bowl, sprinkle the cornstarch over ½ cup of the milk. Whisk to dissolve. Add the sugar and egg yolks and whisk well.

2. In a heavy-bottomed saucepan over medium-low heat, bring the remaining 2 cups milk to a simmer. Pour one third of the hot milk into the yolk mixture and whisk well. Pour the yolk mixture back into the hot milk. Bring it to a full boil, whisking constantly, and cook for about 3 minutes. Remove the saucepan from the heat and add the vanilla. Strain the custard through a fine-mesh sieve into a large bowl and keep warm.

3. To make the hot chocolate, place the chocolate in a heat-proof bowl. Bring the milk to a simmer in a saucepan over medium heat. Pour the hot milk over the chocolate and whisk until smooth. Pour the hot chocolate into the vanilla custard and whisk to combine. Divide the mixture among four mugs and serve hot.

VANILLA CUSTARD

2 tablespoons cornstarch

2½ cups milk

¼ cup sugar

2 egg yolks

1 teaspoon vanilla extract

HOT CHOCOLATE

7 ounces semisweet chocolate, chopped (about 1¼ cups)

1 cup milk

Metric Equivalencies

Liquid and Dry Measure Equivalencies

CUSTOMARY	METRIC
¼ teaspoon	1.25 milliliters
½ teaspoon	2.5 milliliters
1 teaspoon	5 milliliters
1 tablespoon	15 milliliters
1 fluid ounce	30 milliliters
¼ cup	60 milliliters
⅓ cup	80 milliliters
½ cup	120 milliliters
1 cup	240 milliliters
1 pint (2 cups)	480 milliliters
1 quart (4 cups)	960 milliliters (.96 liter)
1 gallon (4 quarts)	3.84 liters
1 ounce (by weight)	28 grams
¼ pound (4 ounces)	114 grams
1 pound (16 ounces)	454 grams
2.2 pounds	1 kilogram (1,000 grams)

Oven-Temperature Equivalencies

DESCRIPTION	°FAHRENHEIT	°CELSIUS
Cool	200	90
Very slow	250	120
Slow	300–325	150–160
Moderately slow	325–350	160–180
Moderate	350–375	180–190
Moderately hot	375–400	190–200
Hot	400–450	200–230
Very hot	450–500	230–260

Index